# CONTENTS

T0342873

# HOW MUCH DO YOU KNOW ALREADY?

**1** The boxes marked a)–g) on the map refer to the following continents. Write these names in the correct boxes on the map.

Africa  Antarctica  Asia  Australia
Europe  North America  South America

**2** Colour these places on the map:

blue = 1 cm square of where the Pacific Ocean is
green = New Zealand
yellow = 1 cm square of where the Tasman Sea is
red = 1 cm square of where the Arctic Ocean is

**3** ①-㉜ on the map refer to the following countries. Write the numbers beside them here.

| | |
|---|---|
| Afghanistan _____ | Israel _____ |
| Argentina _____ | Jamaica _____ |
| Bolivia _____ | Japan _____ |
| Canada _____ | Malaysia _____ |
| China _____ | Myanmar _____ |
| Colombia _____ | Papua New Guinea _____ |
| Egypt _____ | Peru _____ |
| France _____ | Russia _____ |
| Germany _____ | Saudi Arabia _____ |
| Great Britain _____ | Sierra Leone _____ |
| Greece _____ | Singapore _____ |
| Honduras _____ | Solomon Islands _____ |
| India _____ | South Africa _____ |
| Indonesia _____ | Tonga _____ |
| Iraq _____ | USA _____ |
| Italy _____ | Zimbabwe _____ |

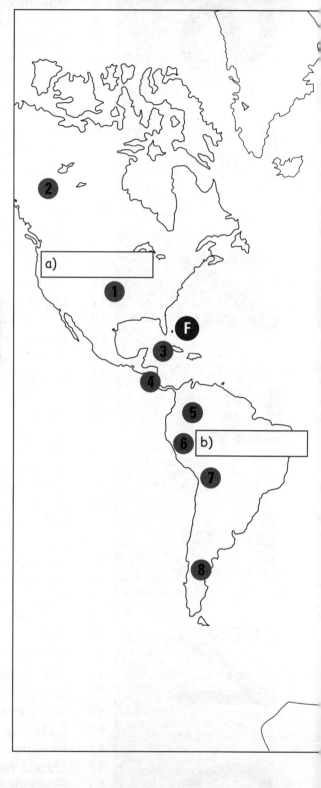

**4** Ⓐ-Ⓖ on the map refer to the following places. Write the letters beside the correct places here.

Balkans _____       Bermuda Triangle _____       Indochina _____       Middle East _____

Monsoon Asia _____       Oceania _____       Sunshine Coast _____

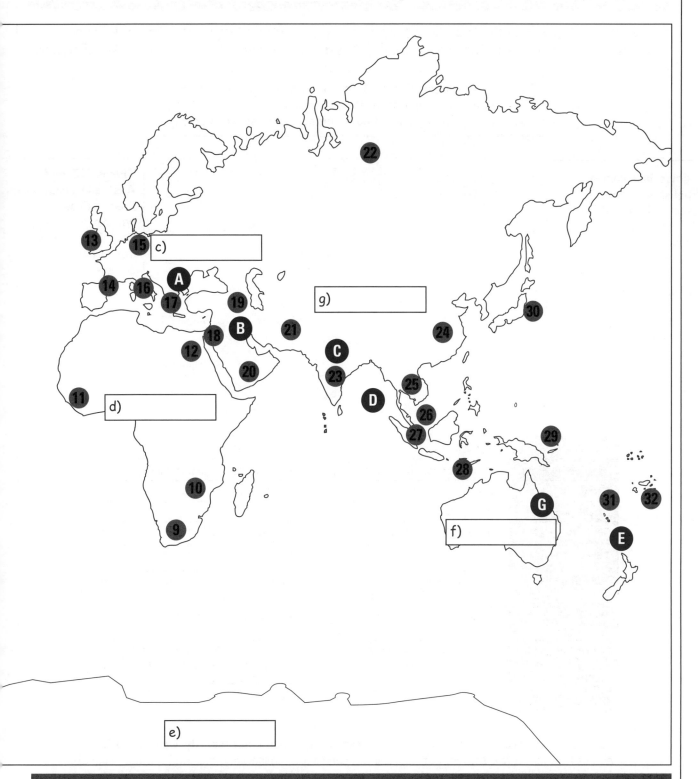

**5** Use the clues in brackets to help you write the following words in the right (approximate) places on the map.

a) BUSHFIRES (every year in country near NZ)
b) US INVASION (in 2003 to topple Saddam Hussein)
c) AIDS EPIDEMIC (in poorest continent in world)
d) SEPTEMBER 2001 (terrorist attacks on New York)
e) KYOTO (place hosted agreement on global warming)
f) EQUATOR (where the imaginary line runs above NZ)
g) COLUMBIA (space shuttle disaster of 2003)
h) KREMLIN (where Moscow's government is)
i) PALESTINIANS (suicide bombers in Israel)
j) OLYMPICS (where the Olympics began)
k) DEMOCRACY (this country is largest democracy in world)

# AUSTRALASIA

Sometimes people include the islands of the Pacific, such as Fiji, Pitcairn and Tonga, when they talk about Australasia. Usually, Australasia means Australia and New Zealand.

In 1901 the six colonies of Australia joined together into the Commonwealth of Australia. Many people on both sides of the Tasman thought NZ should have joined as the seventh colony.

**Things in common:**
English language / used to be ruled by Britain / slang / brandnames / businesses / Anzacs / war histories / sports / majority race are not natives / lifestyles / democracy / possums

**Things NZ and Australia argue over:**
Russell Crowe, pavlova, Phar Lap, Split Enz, Shihad, Jane Campion, Mickey Savage, John Clarke

|  | AUSTRALIA | NEW ZEALAND |
|---|---|---|
| Size | 7,686,850 sq km (incl islands) | 268,680 sq km (incl islands) |
| Coastline | 25,760 km | 15,134 km |
| Population | about 20 million | about 4 million |
| Climate | arid (dry) to semi-arid, temperate (moderate) in south and east, tropical in north | temperate with strong regional differences |
| Terrain | Mostly low plateau with deserts, fertile plain in southeast | largely mountainous with some large coastal plains |
| Natural hazards | cyclone, drought, forest fire | earthquake, volcanic activity, cyclone, flood, drought |
| Ethnic groups | Caucasian 92%, Asian 7%, Aborigine and others 1% | NZ European 74.5%, Maori 9.7%, Other European 4.6%, Pacific Island 3.8%, Asian and others 7.4% |
| GDP per capita | $24,000 | $19,500 |

**Creatures in Australia that Kiwis find interesting but don't necessarily want in NZ:**
bandicoot, black widow spider, buffalo, camel, cane toad, cassowary, crocodile, dingo, funnel-web spider, galah, goanna, great white shark, kangaroo, koala, kookaburra, ostrich, platypus, quoll, red-backed spider, scorpion, snake, Tasmanian devil, tortoise, wombat, yabby

**Write Oz or/and NZ in the boxes to show in which countries the items are more common.**

| | | | |
|---|---|---|---|
| ☐ desert | ☐ cane toad | ☐ mountains | ☐ earthquakes |
| ☐ volcanoes | ☐ Union Jack | ☐ pavlova | ☐ democracy |
| ☐ dingo | ☐ Asians | ☐ English | ☐ Tasman |

# OCEANIA

- The Pacific Ocean is the largest ocean in the world.
- The islands in it are called Oceania.
- There are probably 20,000–30,000 islands but nobody knows exactly.
- The islands range in size from large (Australia) to medium (such as NZ) and small (such as Tonga).
- There are four cultural groups:

1 **Micronesia** (means tiny islands): e.g. Federated states of Micronesia, Palau, Marshall Islands, Nauru, USA dependencies of Guam and Northern Mariana Islands

2 **Melanesia** (means black islands): e.g. Papua New Guinea, Solomon Islands, Vanuatu, Fiji, dependency of New Caledonia (French)

3 **Polynesia** (means many islands): e.g. Kiribati, French Polynesia, Niue, Cook Islands, Pitcairn Island (UK), Hawaii (part of USA), Tonga, Tuvalu, Samoa, dependency of American Samoa (USA)

4 **Australia and NZ**

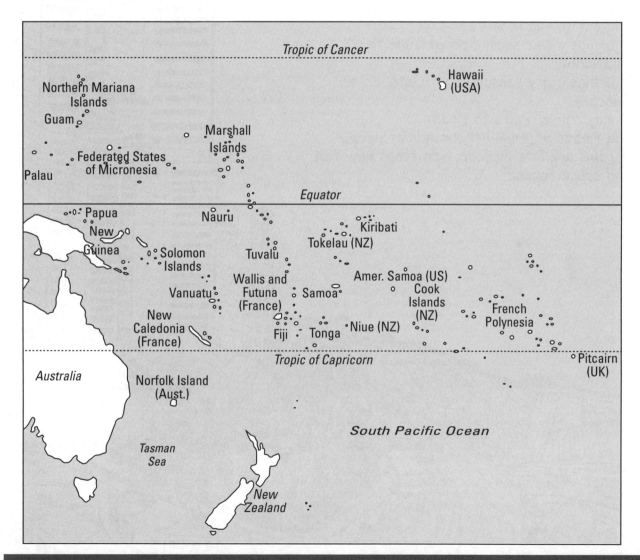

**1** Make the equator line thicker and colour it red. Make the Tropic of Cancer and Tropic of Capricorn lines thicker and colour them green.

**2** Draw lines to show the approximate places of the four cultural groups in Oceania.

Monsoon Asia:
*   is a region of about 21 countries
*   has about 57% of the world's population
*   gets monsoon winds
*   has rainforests, deserts, snowy mountains, hot plains, jungles
*   has rich and poor countries
*   has vast cities and tiny villages
*   has rice as the main crop
*   depends on the monsoon rains for crops to grow.

Monsoon:
*   the word comes from the Arabic 'mawsim' meaning season
*   is a seasonal wind blowing inland in summer and out to sea in winter
*   it brings a wet season about June to September
*   it brings a dry season about October to January
*   it may cause rivers to flood
*   the floods often kill thousands of people
*   if rains are late or poor, rice crops may fail and cause famine.

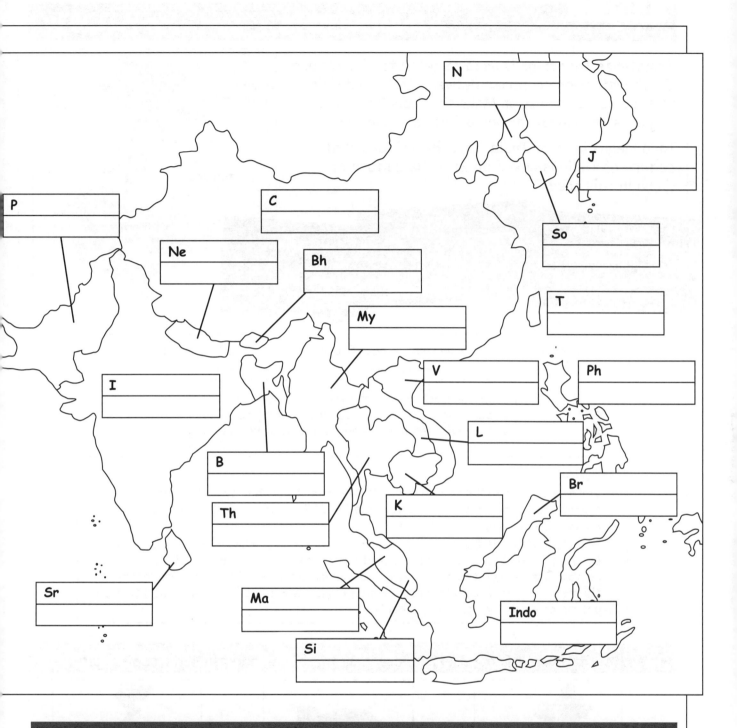

**1** Write the full names of the countries, with their capital cities in brackets (after them) on the map.

| Country | Capital | Country | Capital | Country | Capital |
|---|---|---|---|---|---|
| Bangladesh | Dhaka | Bhutan | Thimphu | Brunei | Bandar Seri Begawan |
| China | Beijing | India | New Delhi | Indonesia | Jakarta |
| Japan | Tokyo | Kampuchea | Phnom Penh | Laos | Vientiane |
| Malaysia | Kuala Lumpur | Myanmar | Yangoon | Nepal | Kathmandu |
| North Korea | Pyongyang | Pakistan | Islamabad | Philippines | Manila |
| Singapore | Singapore | South Korea | Seoul | Sri Lanka | Colombo |
| Taiwan | Taipei | Thailand | Bangkok | Vietnam | Hanoi |

**2** Colour or shade each country differently to its neighbours.

# INDOCHINA

Sometimes Indochina is used to refer to all mainland Southeast Asian countries between India and China (not including peninsular Malaysia). Usually it refers to just Kampuchea/Cambodia, Laos and Vietnam.

Indo means in or of India. Indochina means that the culture of India is mixed up with the culture of China in this area.

Map showing: MYANMAR (Burma), LAOS (Vientiane), THAILAND, Hanoi, VIETNAM, KAMPUCHEA (Cambodia), Phnom Penh

**KAMPUCHEA**
constitutional monarchy
capital = Phnom Penh
produces a lot of tropical rainforest timber

**LAOS**
communist
capital = Vientiane
produces a lot of illegal opium and cannabis

**VIETNAM**
communist
capital = Hanoi
produces a lot of rice

once called French Indochina because France used to rule all three countries

**HAS:** monsoon rains, hot summers, jungle, forest, woods, tigers, leopards, elephants, buffaloes, wild cattle and deer, bears, panthers, poisonous snakes

**HAS HAD:** many wars such as
- Vietnam War of 1950s to 1970s. North Vietnam, supported by Russia and allies, fought against South Vietnam, supported by USA and allies (including NZ) with heavy USA bombing of the North.
- Cambodia in the 1970s. Pol Pot, leader of the Communist Khmer Rouge, seized power. By the time Pol Pot died, he had caused the deaths of more than 2 million Cambodians. He had the professional classes murdered – anyone wearing glasses ran the risk of being killed. He forced people from towns to go into the countryside. He got rid of money and private property.

**1** Write the name of the Indochinese country below and then its capital city.

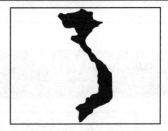

a) _____

_____

b) _____

c) _____

_____

**2** Tick the features that are part of Indochina today.

| | | | |
|---|---|---|---|
| ☐ tigers | ☐ snakes | ☐ heat | ☐ jungle |
| ☐ French rulers | ☐ Pol Pot | ☐ opium | ☐ US bombing |
| ☐ rice | ☐ bears | ☐ panthers | ☐ communism |

# MIDDLE EAST

The East refers to those countries of Asia that lie east of Europe. The Far East refers to countries far east such as China and Japan. The Middle East refers to those countries that lie in the middle – where Africa, Asia and Europe meet.

There is disagreement about exactly which countries belong in the Middle East but often these countries are included.

| COUNTRY | CAPITAL |
| --- | --- |
| Bahrain | Manama |
| Egypt | Cairo |
| Iran | Tehran |
| Iraq | Baghdad |
| Israel | Jerusalem |
| Jordan | Amman |
| Kuwait | Kuwait |
| Lebanon | Beirut |
| Oman | Muscat |
| Palestinian Authority | |
| Qatar | Doha |
| Saudi Arabia | Riyadh |
| Syria | Damascus |
| Turkey | Ankara |
| UAE | Abu Dhabi |
| Yemen | Sana |

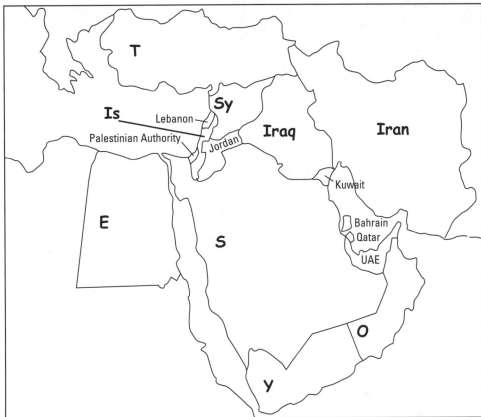

All the countries are different but generally the area has
- a dry climate
- rich petroleum resources
- Islam as the main religion
- shortage of water
- some desalinisation plants (taking salt from water)
- camels, sheep and goats as main livestock.

The area is not united. There have been many conflicts and wars. For example: Israeli/Arab wars; Iraq/Iran war; Iraq/Kuwait wars, unrest in the Kurdish area which is part of Turkey, Iran and Iraq, where the Kurds are fighting off and on to get their own country; US-led invasion to topple Saddam Hussein in Iraq.

## 1 Do detective work to work out names for the following.

a) the capital of the United Arab Emirates _____

b) the area that does not have an official capital city _____

c) the country in Africa _____

d) the resource that experts think may cause future wars _____

e) a group of people who want their own country _____

## 2 Write the full names of all the Middle East countries on the map. Colour in the whole Middle East in one colour.

# UNITED KINGDOM OF GREAT BRITAIN (UK)

The UK is separated by the English Channel from France about 32 km away to the south. A rail tunnel goes under the Channel.

The UK is made up of:
- the large island of Great Britain (often shortened to Britain), which has England in the south with its capital of London, Wales on the west of England with its capital of Cardiff, and Scotland in the north with its capital of Edinburgh
- the far northeast corner of the island of Ireland known as Northern Ireland with its capital of Belfast
- several hundred small islands scattered around the British coast

Overseas territories:
In the 18th and 19th centuries Britain got colonies overseas such as NZ and Australia. This was called the British Empire. Many Kiwis and Aussies go to Britain on working holidays because of these historical links. Today Britain has a few small territories left. They are: Anguilla, Bermuda, British Indian Ocean Territory, British Virgin Islands, Cayman Island, Falkland Island, Gibraltar, Guernsey, Isle of Man, Jersey, Montserrat, Pitcairn Islands, St Helena, South Georgia and the South Sandwich Islands, Turks and Caicos Islands.

Great Britain is a constitutional monarchy. Its royal family is Windsor.

| Queen Elizabeth II |
| m. |

| Charles | Princess Royal | Duke of York | Edward |
| Prince of Wales | m. Mark Phillips | m. Sarah Ferguson | Earl of Wessex |
| m. Lady Diana | div. | div. | m. Sophie Rhys-Jones |
| div. | | | |

**1** Write the following places on the map: England, Scotland, Wales, Northern Ireland, Belfast, Edinburgh, Cardiff, London, English Channel.

**2** Put the following on the Windsor family tree: Philip, Duke of Edinburgh (Elizabeth's husband), Anne (Mark Phillips' ex-wife), Prince William of Wales (elder son of Charles and Diana), Prince Henry of Wales (younger son of Charles and Diana), Andrew (Sarah Ferguson's ex-husband).

# IRELAND AND NORTHERN IRELAND

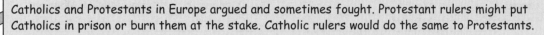

Roman Catholicism is the Christian church headed by the Pope (bishop of Rome). Christians in Europe were Catholics until the 16th century, when the Reformation (reforming or fixing the church) began. It led to a separate Christian religion called Protestantism. Protestants said they didn't need a pope to explain the Bible.

Catholics and Protestants in Europe argued and sometimes fought. Protestant rulers might put Catholics in prison or burn them at the stake. Catholic rulers would do the same to Protestants.

Today Catholics and Protestants still understand Christianity in different ways. Some countries, such as Spain, are almost all Catholic. Some, such as Denmark, are almost all Protestant. Some, such as Switzerland, are half and half.

## Ireland used to be ruled by Britain (UK). It got split into two parts after 1921.

| The Republic of Ireland | Northern Ireland |
|---|---|
| southern 26 counties<br>capital = Dublin<br>main religion = Catholicism<br>rules itself | northern 6 counties<br>capital = Belfast<br>main religion = Protestantism (minority Catholics)<br>stayed part of the United Kingdom which rules it |

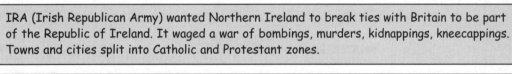

IRA (Irish Republican Army) wanted Northern Ireland to break ties with Britain to be part of the Republic of Ireland. It waged a war of bombings, murders, kidnappings, kneecappings. Towns and cities split into Catholic and Protestant zones.

In the 1960s Catholics in Northern Ireland began a campaign for more civil rights. They said the government stopped them getting good jobs because they were Catholic. British troops arrived to keep the peace but Catholics thought the troops favoured the Protestants. The resulting violence was called The Troubles. Since then the search has been to get Catholics and Protestants living together in permanent peace in Northern Ireland.

**1** Colour the map (Northern Ireland = orange, Republic of Ireland = green)

Belfast

Dublin

**2** Draw and colour these flags.

Republic of Ireland

Northern Ireland

(three equal vertical stripes of, left to right, green, white, orange)

(Union Jack is blue background, red ✚ on white ✚, red X on white X)

**3** Decide if the following are mostly Catholic or mostly Protestant. Write Catholic or Protestant beside them to show this.

a) Northern Ireland _____

b) the Pope _____

c) Christian church before 16th century _____

d) Denmark _____

e) Republic of Ireland _____

f) Spain _____

# THE BALKANS

The Balkans is the name for a group of countries on the Balkan Peninsula, which juts into the Mediterranean Sea. The word Balkan was the Turkish name for a mountain range.

The region is known for its wild and mountainous beauty.

The region used to be ruled by the Turkish Empire. When the Empire broke up, countries were formed but their peoples got muddled up. Different ethnic groups ended up in the same countries, e.g. Serbia was mainly Christian but ended up with some Muslim Albanians.

The countries are Albania, Bosnia and Herzegovina, Croatia, Bulgaria, Greece, Macedonia, Moldova, Romania, Serbia, Montenegro.

Yugoslavia used to include the six republics of Slovenia, Croatia, Bosnia-Herzegovina Macedonia, Serbia and Montenegro. In the 1990s there were ethnic wars and Yugoslavia broke up into separate countries.

The region is called 'the powder keg of Europe' as it often blows up with fighting between ethnic groups.

World War 1 started here in 1914. A young Bosnian killed the heir to the throne of Austria, Archduke Francis Ferdinand, while the Archduke was in the Bosnian capital of Sarajevo. Austria accused Serbia of masterminding the killing. The allies of both sides joined in the argument and war began.

In 1998 fighting erupted between Serbs and Albanians in Kosova, a province of Serbia. As a result, NATO (North Atlantic Treaty Organisation) bombed Yugoslavia for 78 days. Later the Serbian government handed Yugoslav President Milosevic over to the War Crimes Tribunal in The Hague to be tried for crimes against humanity.

## 1 Colour in the map.

a) countries known as the Balkans = red
b) other countries = colour of your choice

## 2 Tick or cross the boxes to show whether they are part of the present-day Balkans or not.

| | | | |
|---|---|---|---|
| ☐ Austria | ☐ Romania | ☐ Slovenia | ☐ Francis Ferdinand |
| ☐ Italy | ☐ NATO | ☐ Bulgaria | ☐ Sarajevo |
| ☐ Kosovo | ☐ Bosnia | ☐ Albania | ☐ Turkish Empire |

# Unit 10

# RUSSIA AND THE OLD USSR

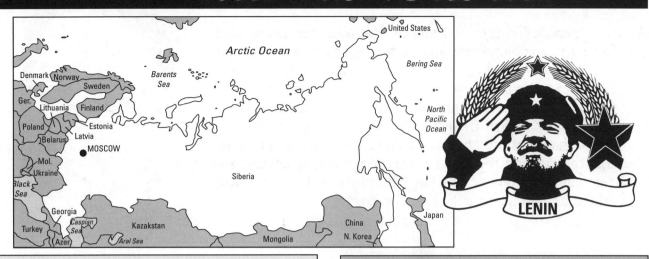

**Russia**
- its capital is Moscow
- it's a federal republic (the head is a president)
- it's the largest country in the world (almost twice the size of the USA)
- it takes up the eastern part of Europe and the whole of northern Asia

For about 70 years, until 1991, Russia was part of communist USSR (Union of Soviet Socialist Republics). Soviet means council, and socialist means the community owning and controlling land and other resources.

**Some leaders of the USSR**
- Lenin – 'father of communism'
- Stalin – had millions of people who opposed him killed
- Kruschchev – almost started a war with the USA when he tried to put nuclear weapons on Cuba
- Gorbachev – relaxed the 'rules' of communism that led to the breakup of the USSR

After World War 2 ended in 1945, the world had two superpowers – USSR and USA. Although they avoided war, they did not trust each other and both sides built up nuclear weapons. This was called the Cold War as it was a war of words. It was the time of spies, early James Bond movies, and the Iron Curtain (an imaginary line between the USSR and its friends in the Warsaw Pact, and the USA and its friends in NATO).

In 1991 the USSR broke up. It was replaced by the Commonwealth of Independent States (CIS) made up of some former Soviet republics.

Russia is trying to get full democracy working. It has had many bad disasters such as the sinking of the Kursk nuclear submarine, which saw 118 crew die after explosions on board. Its war against Chechnya, a province that Russia says is part of Russia, but which wants its independence, caused the Chechens to stage 'terrorist' attacks inside Russia.

**1** In the box, draw and colour in the flag of Russia. [three equal horizontal bands of white (top), blue and red]

**2** Write down the name of the following.

a) a cruel ruler _____

b) NATO's opposition _____

c) people from Chechnya _____

d) submarine disaster _____

e) leader during Cuban missile crisis _____

f) old group of soviets _____

**3** Write down the names of nine of Russia's closest neighbours.

_____  _____  _____

_____  _____  _____

_____  _____  _____

# AFRICA

Africa is separated from Europe by the Mediterranean Sea and from the Arabian Peninsula on the east by the Red Sea and the Suez Canal, which connects the Mediterranean and Red Seas. It is bounded by the Atlantic Ocean to the west and the Indian Ocean to the east. The Sahara Desert is in the north and Kalahari Desert is in the south. It is the only continent that has the tropics of Cancer and Capricorn and the equator running through it. The Congo Basin, around the equator, supports one of the largest rainforests in the world. The island of Madagascar lies to the east.

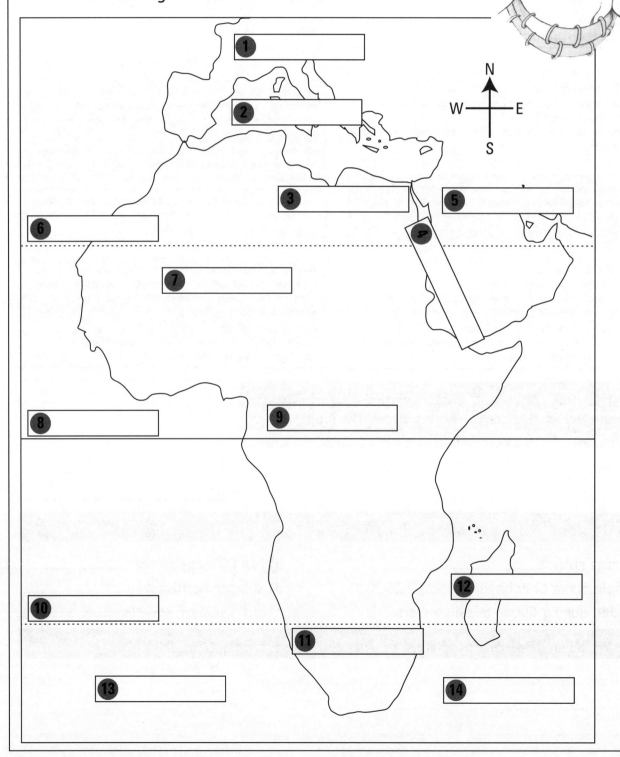

**Africa covers about one fifth of the Earth's land. Its countries are:**

·Algeria ·Angola ·Benin ·Botswana ·Burkina Faso ·Burundi ·Cameroon ·Cape Verde ·Central African Republic ·Chad ·Comoros ·Congo ·Congo, Democratic Republic of ·Cote d'Ivoire ·Djibouti ·Egypt ·Equatorial Guinea ·Eritrea ·Ethiopia ·Gabon ·Gambia ·Ghana ·Guinea ·Guinea-Bissau ·Kenya ·Lesotho ·Liberia ·Libya ·Madagascar ·Malawi ·Mali ·Mauritania ·Mauritius ·Morocco ·Mozambique ·Namibia ·Niger ·Nigeria ·Rwanda ·Sao Tome and Principe ·Senegal ·Seychelles ·Sierra Leone ·Somalia ·South Africa ·Sudan ·Swaziland ·Tanzania ·Togo ·Tunisia ·Uganda ·Zambia ·Zimbabwe

**Excitement plus:**
The big differences in peoples, cultures, languages, religions, population, climate, landscapes and wildlife make Africa a great place for tourists to visit.

**Land grab:**
In the late 19th century almost all Africa was claimed by countries in Europe such as Britain, France and Germany.

**Independence:**
In the 20th century African countries struggled to get free of their European rulers.

**Exploration:**
Europeans used to call Africa 'the dark continent' because they didn't know much about it. It was hard to explore because of big surf and few sheltered harbours, rapids and waterfalls on its rivers, dense forest and coastal mangrove swamps, and hard climate. Europeans didn't explore it until the late 18th century.

**Africa's Big Problems**

1 has largest number of the poorest countries in the world
2 only continent where economic production per person has gone down
3 primitive technology for agriculture
4 when it doesn't rain there is drought and famine
5 when it rains too much there are floods and famine
6 many countries do not have democracy
7 women treated as second-class citizens even though they grow most of food
8 many countries have difficulty feeding their people
9 trees cut down for household fuel, to make farms, to sell for timber
10 giant share of world's population but dwarf share of world trade
11 some African countries owe huge amounts of money to the IMF
12 AIDS is spreading fast
13 desertification (land becoming desert)
14 some countries are fighting bloody civil wars
15 some countries fight wars with their neighbours
16 much land is poor, overworked
17 overseas aid often arrives too late and gets tied up with red tape
18 life expectancies are low – 52 years for males, 55 years for females
19 few countries have much industry
20 endangered animals such as African hunting dog, pygmy hippo, mountain gorilla, Nile crocodile, black rhino, goliath frog, giant sable antelope

---

**1** In the boxes on the map, write the names of the following:

a) the continent at **1**
b) the seas at **2** **4**
c) the waterway at **3**
d) the land mass at **5**
e) the 'lines' at **6** **8** **10**
f) the deserts at **7** **11**
g) the basin at **9**
h) the land at **12**
i) the oceans at **13** **14**

---

**2** Add together: the number of African countries listed, male life expectancy, the century of exploration, and the century of independence-fighting.

TOTAL: 

---

**3** Write down the numbers belonging to 'Africa's Big Problems' that are:

a) mainly political _____

b) mainly agricultural _____

c) mainly about health _____

# KIWIS ON OE

Many young Kiwis and Aussies go on an OE (overseas experience). They are said to be from down-under (NZ and Australia seen from the northern hemisphere). They often head for traditional attractions:

tour = travel from place to place
tourist = person who tours

Acropolis (Greece), Anne Frank House (Netherlands), Blue Mosque (Turkey), bull running (Pamplona/Spain), channel tunnel (UK/France), Colosseum (Italy), Eiffel Tower (France), Everest Base Camp Trail (Nepal), Golden Gate Bridge (San Francisco US), Grand Canyon (US), Great Barrier Reef (Australia), Great Wall of China, Iguaçu Falls (Argentina/Brazil), Kruger National Park (South Africa), Leaning Tower of Pisa (Italy), Loch Ness monster (Scotland), Marrakech markets (Morocco), mountain gorillas (Rwanda), Neuschwanstein castle (Germany), Niagara Falls (Canada/US), Norwegion Fjords (Norway), opera house (Sydney), pyramids (Egypt), Rio Mardi Gras (Brazil), Rockies (Canada), State Hermitage museum (St Petersburg), statues (Easter Island), Statue of Liberty (New York, US), Taj Mahal (India), Tower of London (UK)

**1** Write into the key on page 17 the country where each tourist attraction is located.

**2** Write the number of each tourist attraction into its correct location on this map.

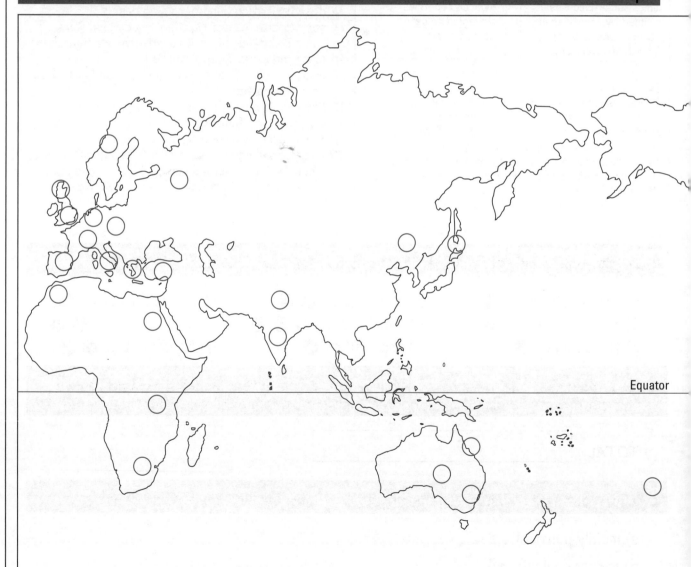

Equator

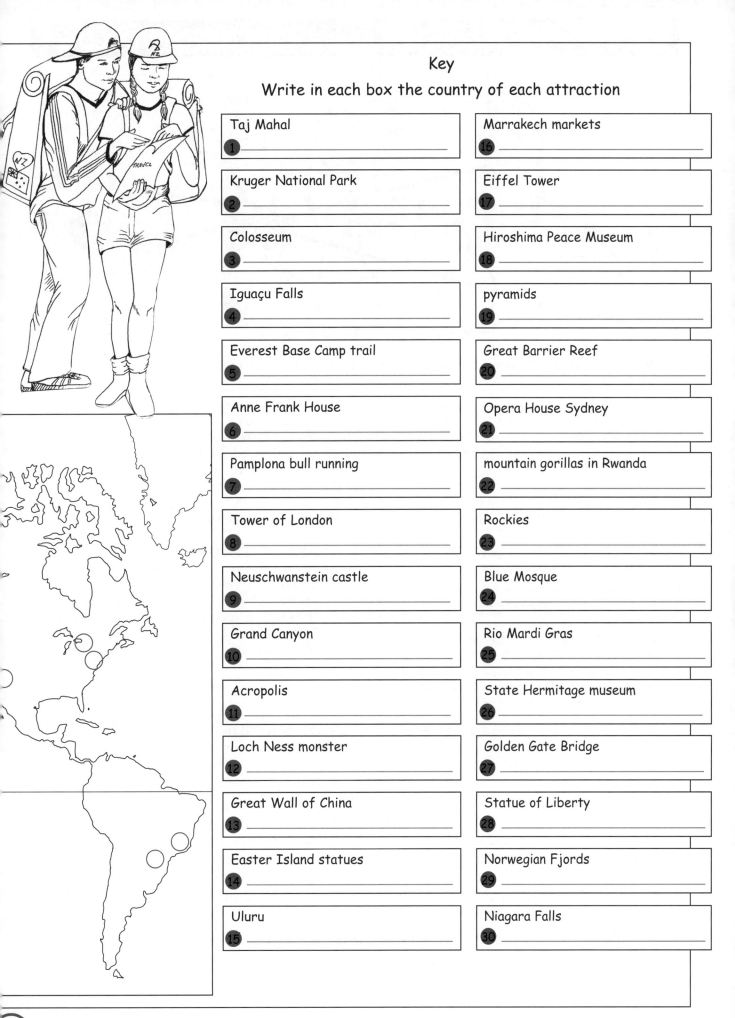

# Key

## Write in each box the country of each attraction

Taj Mahal
1 _____

Kruger National Park
2 _____

Colosseum
3 _____

Iguaçu Falls
4 _____

Everest Base Camp trail
5 _____

Anne Frank House
6 _____

Pamplona bull running
7 _____

Tower of London
8 _____

Neuschwanstein castle
9 _____

Grand Canyon
10 _____

Acropolis
11 _____

Loch Ness monster
12 _____

Great Wall of China
13 _____

Easter Island statues
14 _____

Uluru
15 _____

Marrakech markets
16 _____

Eiffel Tower
17 _____

Hiroshima Peace Museum
18 _____

pyramids
19 _____

Great Barrier Reef
20 _____

Opera House Sydney
21 _____

mountain gorillas in Rwanda
22 _____

Rockies
23 _____

Blue Mosque
24 _____

Rio Mardi Gras
25 _____

State Hermitage museum
26 _____

Golden Gate Bridge
27 _____

Statue of Liberty
28 _____

Norwegian Fjords
29 _____

Niagara Falls
30 _____

# DEVELOPING AND DEVELOPED WORLDS

People use special terms to show whether a country is a rich or poor country.

**THIRD WORLD:** This term started when the world had two superpowers. Democratic US was the First World. Communist Soviet Union (now broken into Russia and other countries) was the Second World. Third World countries were those that were not aligned to (friends with) either the First or Second World, and also countries who got their independence from other countries after WW2 (1939-45). But a country such as Singapore, which got its independence from Britain and is rich, has little in common with a country such as Chad, which got its independence from France and is poor. So Third World is not a good term.

**NORTH (richer countries) and SOUTH (poorer countries):** This does not make total sense. Australia and NZ, for example, are in the South. Yet they are rich countries.

**WEST or WESTERN COUNTRIES:** This means rich industrialised countries. It usually includes US, Canada, much of Europe, Australia, NZ, Japan, South Korea, Taiwan, Israel. It usually does not include mainland China, most of the Middle East, India, Russia, Latin America, South America.

**INDUSTRIALISED WORLD and NON-INDUSTRIALISED WORLD:** Industrialised countries have more industry (factories and technology) than non-industrialised countries.

**DEVELOPED WORLD and DEVELOPING WORLD:** These are better terms. Developed means countries that are industry-rich and technology-rich. Developing means countries that are on their way (hopefully) to becoming industry-rich and technology-rich.

About 80% of the world is developing and these features are common: high illiteracy (people who can't read and write)/many diseases/low life expectancy/poor health care/high population growth/many people living below the poverty line/high infant mortality rate/unable to cope with extreme hazards such as drought, floods and famine/unstable government/lack of democracy/peasant farmers/huge debt/depend on exporting primary goods to developed countries.

About 20% of the world is developed and these features are common: high standard of living/democracy/military alliances with each other/high levels of education/share much popular culture.

**1** Write down four terms to describe countries that are industry-poor and technology-poor.

a) _____    c) _____

b) _____    d) _____

**2** Write down four terms to describe countries that are industry-rich and technology-rich.

a) _____    c) _____

b) _____    d) _____

**3** Colour red the boxes beside countries that are probably developing and colour blue the boxes beside countries that are probably developed.

| | | |
|---|---|---|
| ☐ Australia (Pacific) | ☐ Somalia (Africa) | ☐ Canada (North America) |
| ☐ Nepal (Asia) | ☐ Haiti (Latin America) | ☐ Gambia (Africa) |
| ☐ NZ (Pacific) | ☐ Finland (Europe) | ☐ Afghanistan (Asia) |
| ☐ Germany (Europe) | ☐ Ethiopia (Africa) | ☐ Honduras (Latin America) |
| ☐ France (Europe) | ☐ Peru (South America) | ☐ Tonga (Pacific) |

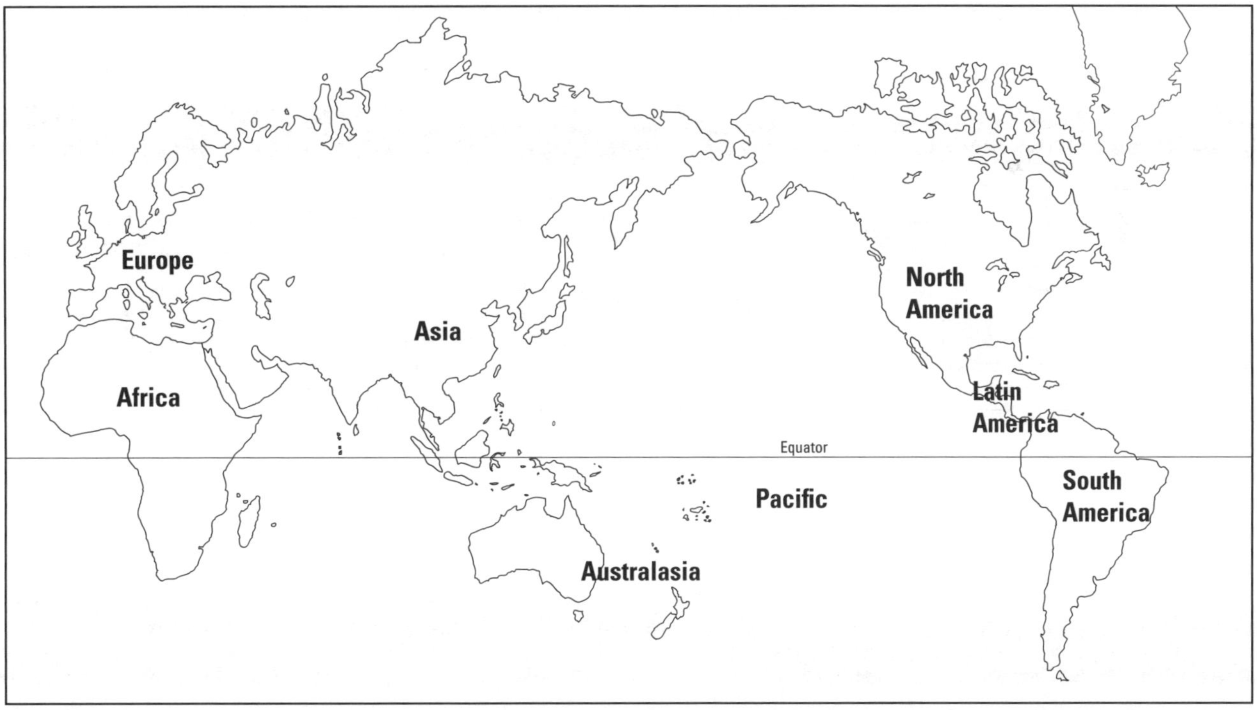

Europe

Asia

Africa

North America

Latin America

Equator

Pacific

South America

Australasia

**4** Write down four ways poor countries help rich countries stay rich.

_____

_____

_____

# DIFFERENT GOVERNMENTS

**democracy** = people vote for who they want to represent them in government, e.g. NZ, Australia, USA

**communism** = economic activity is carried out by the state under one political party, the communist party, e.g. Cuba

**republic** = country that does not have a king or queen; often has a president as its head, e.g. USA, Indonesia

**federation** = different states have their own governments and also join together under one central government, e.g. Australia, USA

**totalitarianism** = a single party or a dictator has absolute power, e.g. Iraq when ruled by Saddam Hussein

**theocracy** = a church or religious group is in charge of government, e.g. in 2002 Afghanistan got rid of its theocracy, which was a very strict Muslim sect known as the Taleban

## Examples of nicknames for governments

**Big Brother** = a dictator, comes from a character in a novel *1984* by George Orwell

**White House** = where the US president lives in Washington, symbol of president and US government

**Westminster** = British Parliament is situated in the borough of Westminster in London, symbol for British Parliament

**Whitehall** = a street in Westminster that has many government offices, symbol for the British government

**Pentagon** = Headquarters of US Department of Defense in Washington (a pentagon is a polygon with five angles and five sides); a nickname for US government's military decision-makers

**Kremlin** = Russian 'Kreml' means citadel (fortress), symbol for Russian government in Moscow

**Beehive** = NZ Parliament in Wellington (from shape of building housing government offices)

## 1 Write in the names of the buildings and the cities in which they are found.

a) _____   b) _____   c) _____   d) _____   e) _____

_____ _____ _____ _____ _____

## 2 Use the clues to work out which term best fits these countries. Terms = theocracy, democracy, communist.

a) North Korea (has same system of government as Cuba) _____

b) India (largest one of its kind in the world, holds elections for government)

_____

c) Iran (has same system of government as Afghanistan used to)

_____

### Examples of different terms used by countries for their 'parliaments'

Britain = House of Lords and House of Commons
Israel = Knesset
China = National People's Congress
USA = Senate and House of Representatives
NZ = House of Representatives
Chile = High Assembly and Chamber of Deputies
Botswana = House of Chiefs and National Assembly
Sweden = Riksdag
Russia = Federation Council and State Duma
Taiwan = National Assembly and Legislative Yuan
Saudi Arabia = Monarchy with Advisory Consultative Council
Jordan = House of Notables and House of Representatives
Japan = House of Councillors and House of Representatives
Lebanon = National Assembly
Singapore = Parliament

### Different names for royalty

**Crowned Head**, **King** or **Queen**, **Majesty**, **Royal Highness**, **Monarch**, **Tsar** and **Tsarina** (names of the rulers of Russia before the communists took over), **Sovereign**, **Rex** or **Regina**, **Sultan** (Muslim), **Emperor** or **Empress**, **Emir** (chief or prince who rules in a Muslim country)
**traditional monarchy** = king or queen has absolute power, e.g. Bahrain
**constitutional monarchy** = government has the real power, e.g. Britain

### Different names for leaders of governments

**Prime Minister** e.g. NZ
**President** e.g. USA
**Premier** e.g. China
**Chancellor** e.g. Germany
**Dictator** = leader with unlimited power, who often has taken control by force, e.g. Adolf Hitler in Nazi Germany
**Tyrant** = cruel unjust leader, e.g. President Saddam Hussein of Iraq

---

**Use the clues in brackets to help you write the terms in the right place.**
**TERMS: Czar, Parliament, Dictator, Sultan, House of Representatives, President, National Assembly, Tyrant, Senate**

a) Brunei's leader (one of the richest men in world, leads Islamic sultanate) _____

b) Russian emperor (alternative spelling for ruler in old Russia) _____

c) One of Australia's two government bodies (has same as NZ's) _____

d) Joseph Stalin (cruel and unjust former Russian leader) _____

e) Sri Lanka's government body (same as Singapore's) _____

f) South Korea's government body (same as Lebanon's) _____

g) Thailand's bodies of government (same as USA) _____ and _____

h) Benito Mussolini (former Italian leader who seized power) _____

i) Argentine leader (same as leader of USA) _____

# COMMONWEALTH OF NATIONS

The Commonwealth has about 54 member countries. (Countries can get suspended and expelled. For example, Nigeria was suspended after it executed a writer, and Fiji was suspended after its elected government was overthrown by force.)

**Members today (30% of the world's population)**
Antigua and Barbuda, Australia, Bahamas, Bangladesh, Barbados, Belize, Botswana, Brunei Darussalam, Cameroon, Canada, Cyprus, Dominica, Fiji, Gambia, Ghana, Grenada, Guyana, India, Jamaica, Kenya, Kiribati, Lesotho, Malawi, Malaysia, Maldives, Malta, Mauritius, Mozambique, Namibia, Nauru, New Zealand, Nigeria, Pakistan (suspended), Papua New Guinea, Samoa, Seychelles, Sierra Leone, Singapore, Solomon Islands, South Africa, Sri Lanka, St Kitts and Nevis, St Lucia, St Vincent and The Grenadines, Swaziland, United Republic of Tanzania, Tonga, Trinidad and Tobago, Tuvalu, Uganda, United Kingdom, Vanuatu, Zambia, Zimbabwe (suspended)

People who want to keep the British Royal family are called **monarchists**; people who don't are called **republicans**.

About the Commonwealth:
- grew out of British Empire (Britain used to rule many countries such as NZ and Australia)
- members have historical ties with Britain (except Mozambique, which doesn't)
- known as the Family of Nations
- many members recognise the head of the British Royal Family as their Head of State
- its Secretary-General is chosen by members (e.g. Don McKinnon from NZ, 2000–2005)
- the second Monday in March is Commonwealth Day
- members share sports such as cricket; Commonwealth Games every four years
- members share a common language – English
- members help each other with skills and technological ideas
- CHOGM (Commonwealth Heads of Government Meeting) every two years
- works to get rid of poverty in member countries and help their economies
- gives scholarships for students to study in other countries
- puts pressure on countries that go away from democracy
- puts pressure on countries that break human rights laws

**1** Four countries that have been suspended from the Commonwealth are:

a) _____  b) _____  c) _____  d) _____

**2** Write in the name or term for the following.

a) the one member country with no historical ties to Britain _____

b) second Monday in March _____

c) old group where Britain used to rule member countries _____

d) meeting of Heads of State every two years _____

e) held every four years _____

f) person in favour of keeping Royal Family as Head of State _____

g) person against keeping Royal Family as Head of State _____

h) chosen by members for five-year term _____

# Unit 17 — UNITED NATIONS (UN)

UN was set up in 1945, after WW2, to:
- stop wars
- develop friendship among countries
- get security and peace in the world
- solve global problems
- sort out arguments between countries
- get human rights everywhere
- make life better for people.

The UN has three main parts

[1] General Assembly → meets once a year to talk about things happening in the world, but can meet more often if there is a crisis; each member has one vote

[2] Security Council → has five permanent members (China, France, UK, USA, Russia) and a rotation system for 10 non-permanent members drawn alphabetically

[3] Special organisations →

Examples:
**FAO** (Food and Agriculture Organisation)
**WHO** (World Health Organisation)
**IMF** (International Monetary Fund)
**UNICEF** (UN International Children's Emergency Fund, now called UN Children's Fund)
**UNESCO** (UN Educational, Scientific and Cultural Organisation)
**IAEA** (International Atomic Energy Agency)
**World Court** (sits at The Hague in Netherlands)

- Any country can join UN if it agrees with the aims.
- World HQ are on New York's East River in the United States.
- European HQ are in Geneva, Switzerland.
- UN has its own flag and postage stamps.
- UN can send observer or peace-keeping forces to war zones and trouble spots.

**1** Draw arrows to show the position on the UN logo (above) of these:

   a) olive branches (for peace)  b) continents (for where people live)  c) globe (for world)

**2** Name the place where the following are found.

   a) World HQ of UN _____  b) World Court _____
   c) European HQ of UN _____

**3** Write the full names for these organisations.

   a) UN _____  b) FAO _____
   c) WHO _____  d) UNICEF _____
   e) IAEA _____  f) UNESCO _____

**4** Work out to which UN organisation this logo would belong.

_____

# HUMAN RIGHTS AND AMNESTY INTERNATIONAL (AI)

The Universal Declaration of Human Rights:
- was set up in 1948 by the United Nations
- has 30 rights that belong to you and every other person in the world, no matter who or what you are.
- Every one of the 30 rights is violated (broken) somewhere in the world every day.

**universal** = worldwide
**declaration** = statement
**right** = fair claim or title
**human rights** = rights every human has

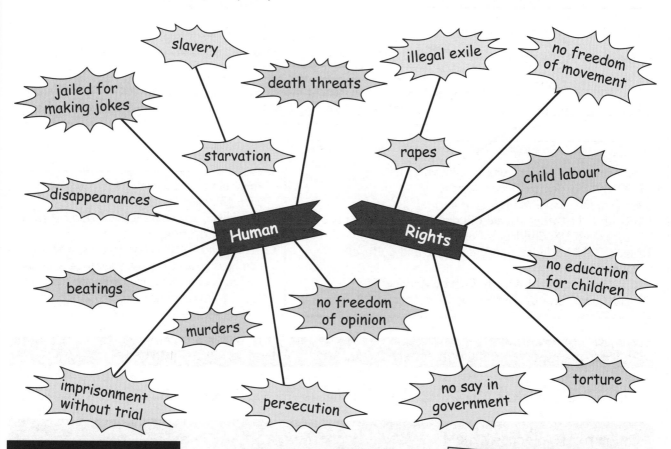

slavery · jailed for making jokes · death threats · illegal exile · no freedom of movement · starvation · rapes · child labour · disappearances · **Human** · **Rights** · beatings · no freedom of opinion · no education for children · murders · imprisonment without trial · persecution · no say in government · torture

## Amnesty International

- began in London, England in 1961
- now has over a million members from all over the world
- researches violations (breakings) of human rights
- members put pressure on governments, especially by writing letters and emails, to free POCs, end torture, get fair trials for political prisoners, stop political murders and 'disappearances', and get rid of the death penalty around the world
- anyone can join – lots of schoolchildren write letters for AI

**amnesty** = a pardon, especially for 'crimes' against a government
**international** = worldwide
**POCs** = prisoners of conscience = people who suffer for their beliefs and often held without trial for a long time

Results of AI pressure:
- POCs released from prison
- government officials put on trial for human rights abuses
- better treatment for people accused of crimes
- death sentences commuted (made less severe, e.g. to life imprisonment)
- official enquiries into human rights abuses

**1** Draw and colour the AI logo (candle and barbed wire).

**2** Draw and colour the bird associated most with AI.

**3** Write down the term that best matches the following.

a) applying force _____    b) make less severe _____

c) pardon _____    d) fair claim _____

e) break _____    f) statement _____

g) worldwide _____    h) worldwide _____

i) use wrongly _____    j) tells you right from wrong _____

# CLUBS FOR COUNTRIES

Countries belong to clubs with other countries to help with their trade, economic development and defence. Here are some of them:

**ANZUS** = Australia, New Zealand, United States
- defence security pact for the Pacific
- set up in 1951
- if another country attacked an ANZUS country, the other two did not have to give military help but would be available for talks about the attack
- in the 1980s NZ had a nuclear-free policy and when US refused to confirm or deny whether its ships wanting to come to NZ ports were nuclear, NZ banned them from coming
- this resulted in NZ being suspended from ANZUS

**APEC** = Asia Pacific Economic Cooperation
- 21 members including Australia and NZ
- aims to help trade, security and standards of living in the region

**ASEAN** = Association of Southeast Asian Nations
- Australia and NZ are not members but they work closely with members
- e.g. the Five Power Defence Arrangements to help keep peace in the region is made up of Malaysia, Singapore, Britain, Australia and NZ

**CER** = short for ANZCERTA = Australian New Zealand Closer Economic Relations Trade Agreement
- aims to help trade and economic relations between Australia and NZ

**G77** (Group of 77)
- set up by 77 developing countries
- membership has since increased to 133 but they've kept the original name (NZ and Australia are not members)
- aims to help economies of its members

**EU** = European Union
- 15 members in Europe
- aims to bring countries closer, and lift standards of living
- 12 of the countries in 2002 introduced euro notes and coins to replace national currencies, e.g. euro replaced Greek drachmas and Spanish pesetas

**G8** (Group of 8)
- members are France, US, Britain, Germany, Japan, Italy, Canada, Russia
- also includes the European Community
- aims to get economic and political cooperation

**IMF** (International Monetary Fund)
- 184 member countries (includes NZ and Australia)
- aims to smooth out money matters, to get economic growth and jobs, and to lend money to poorer countries

**NATO** (North Atlantic Treaty Organisation)
- members are Belgium, Canada, Czech Republic, Denmark, France, Germany, Greece, Hungary, Iceland, Italy, Luxembourg, Netherlands, Norway, Poland, Portugal, Spain, Turkey, United Kingdom, USA
- military alliance of democratic countries in Europe and North America

**OECD** (Organisation for Economic Cooperation and Development)
- members are Australia, Austria, Belgium, Canada, Czech Republic, Denmark, Finland, France, Germany, Greece, Hungary, Iceland, Ireland, Italy, Japan, South Korea, Luxembourg, Mexico, Netherlands, NZ, Norway, Poland, Portugal, Slovakia, Spain, Sweden, Switzerland, Turkey, United Kingdom, USA
- aims to have an organisation for countries that believe in democracy and a free market economy
- it does a lot of research and publishes statistics
- most members are industrialised and wealthy, so it is nicknamed the 'rich man's club'

**PIF** = Pacific Island Forum
- has Pacific member countries including NZ and Australia
- forum = place to talk
- members meet to talk about issues such as trade, the environment, global warming, fisheries

**SPARTECA** = South Pacific Regional Trade and Economic Cooperation Agreement
- is about the South Pacific including NZ and Australia
- aims to fix up the unequal trade relationships of NZ and Australia with small countries in the Pacific
- imports from South Pacific countries to go in duty-free to NZ and Australia

**WORLD BANK**
- owned by 183 member countries including NZ and Australia
- lends money to developing countries
- aims to reduce poverty, protect the environment, improve living standards

Clients of the World Bank
- 4.7 billion people
- 3 billion live on less than $2 a day
- 1.2 billion live on less than $1 a day
- 1.5 billion do not have clean water to drink
- about 3 million children die each year from vaccine-preventable diseases
- 113 million children are not in school

**UNSCOM** = United Nations Special Commission
- set up after the Gulf War in 1991 when the world realised that Iraq's unconventional weaponry was growing and its programmes to develop nuclear, chemical and biological weapons were seen as a threat to world security
- aimed to check out and get rid of Iraq's chemical and biological weapons and its ballistic missiles with a range greater than 150 km
- was to carry out on-site inspections of Iraq's chemical, biological and missile capabilities

**WTO** = World Trade Organisation
- has 144 member countries including NZ and Australia
- is a trade treaty
- provides rules and a forum for countries to talk about and fix trade problems

**1** Write what the following stand for and in the boxes beside each one tick or cross to show if Australia and NZ are members or not.

☐ a) APEC _____

☐ b) ASEAN _____

☐ c) CER _____

☐ d) EU _____

☐ e) G77 _____

☐ f) G8 _____

☐ g) NATO _____

☐ h) IMF _____

☐ i) OECD _____

**2** Check out the drawing.

a) The organisation whose membership matches/matched the drawing is

_____.

b) The original members were _____,

_____ and _____.

c) The suspended member is _____.

d) The reason for the suspension was

_____.

# BUDDHISM

Buddha was born c 566 BC, and died c 486 BC. The name Buddha means "The One Who Knows". The Buddha's name was Siddhartha. He was a prince of a tribe in India. As a young man he wanted to discover the meaning of life and help people overcome suffering. One day he sat under a bodhi-tree, a wild fig tree, and waited until he found his answer. Then he wandered India teaching the answer. Buddhists kneel before the image of Buddha. This is not in worship or prayer because they don't worship God. It is in meditation (thinking) on Buddha's teaching.

Buddhist beliefs
- there are eight 'right' principles to follow – beliefs, aims, speech, conduct, occupation, effort, thinking, meditation
- meditation develops more positive states of mind such as calmness, concentration, awareness, friendliness, non-violence, tolerance of differences
- the aim is to reach nirvana – a state of perfect peace with no suffering
- when people die they will later be born again
- life events are punishment or reward for things done in an earlier life
- earlier actions are known as karma
- good deeds and meditation can wipe out bad karma and bring nirvana
- it is wrong to take any kind of life as all life is sacred

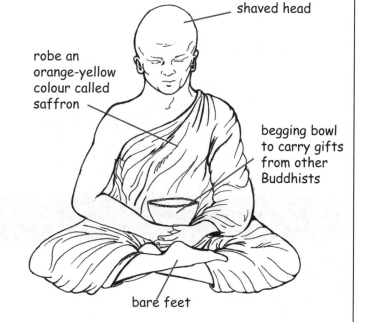

shaved head

robe an orange-yellow colour called saffron

begging bowl to carry gifts from other Buddhists

bare feet

**Top Buddhism regions**
- Thailand
- Bhutan
- Laos
- Macau
- Kampuchea
- Sri Lanka
- Vietnam
- Taiwan
- Myanmar
- Tibet
- Japan

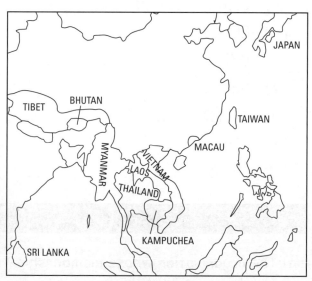

JAPAN

TIBET    BHUTAN

TAIWAN

BHUTAN

MACAU

TIBET

MYANMAR

VIETNAM

LAOS

THAILAND

KAMPUCHEA

SRI LANKA

**1** On the map colour in one colour the top Buddhist regions.

**2** Circle the 10 words that best describe Buddhism.

| | | | | |
|---|---|---|---|---|
| calmness | looks | travelling | technology | |
| kindness | adventure | frantic | partying | |
| violence | wisdom | tolerance | understanding | |
| speed | winning | positive | money | |
| friendliness | peace | competition | nirvana | karma |

Christians believe that God visited Earth in the person of Jesus Christ to fix the mess people had made of their lives. The idea was to show people what God was like and the kind of life they should live.

Jesus Christ was a Jew who lived about 2000 years ago in the area where Israel is today.

Christians believe Jesus was the Son of God. Jews do not.

Jews were frightened of the influence of Jesus. They got Pontius Pilate, the Roman Governor who ruled the region, to put Jesus to death. Jesus was accused of being an anti-government rebel. He was crucified – nailed to a cross and left to die. Later he rose from the dead and ascended into Heaven.

**Some Christian denominations (versions)**
- Apostolic · Brethren
- Christian Scientist · Anglican
- Congregationalist · Mormon
- Jehovah's Witness · Baptist
- Methodist · Orthodox
- Latter-day Saints
- Pentecostal · Presbyterian
- Roman Catholic · Wesleyan
- Salvation Army

Christians believe:

- The Bible is the Word of God. (Both Jews and Christians accept the Old Testament part of the Bible, but only Christians accept the New Testament part of the Bible.)

- There is only one God. He is three persons: Father, Son and Holy Spirit.

- God created all people, the world, the universe, and everything in it.

- Jesus Christ is the Son of God and is One with God.

- Jesus Christ died on the cross for people's sins, was buried, rose again from the dead, ascended back to Heaven, and will one day return to Earth.

- People who are sorry for their sins will be forgiven.

- People who have faith in Jesus Christ will have eternal life.

---

**1** Write in the boxes the numbers of the events that are illustrated.

a) [ ]　　b) [ ]　　c) [ ]　　d) [ ]　　e) [ ]　　f) [ ]

**1** Jesus was born in Bethlehem. (Christmas)　**2** Jesus was crucified. (Good Friday)　**3** Jesus entered Jerusalem on a donkey. (Palm Sunday)　**4** The tomb where Jesus was buried was found empty. (Easter Sunday)　**5** Jesus spent 40 days in the desert fasting and praying.　**6** After the death of Jesus, disciples spread the message.

---

**2** Circle which religions come under the umbrella of Christianity.

| | | | | | |
|---|---|---|---|---|---|
| Judaism | Presbyterianism | Anglicanism | Taoism | Shintoism | Methodism |
| Islam | Roman Catholicism | Baptist | Hinduism | Sikhism | Baha'ism |

# HINDUISM

Hinduism is an old religion that began in India. Most Hindus live in India although Hindus are found in all countries.

Hindus also worship other gods such as Vishnu (who preserves life and is reborn on Earth from time to time to fight evil and protect humankind), Shiva (the destroyer who stands for all the forces of nature), Saraswati (goddess of learning), Lakshmi (goddess of wealth), and Ganesha (who is very fat with an elephant's head, and is the remover of obstacles).

Certain rivers are sacred and can wash away sins, e.g. the Ganges River, which has the holy city of Varanasi on its banks. Also sacred are certain animals such as the cow, monkey, peacock, squirrel and cobra snake.

Hindus had a caste system where everyone was given a place in society depending on their job. The bottom people were the Untouchables or Dalit. They worked at polluting jobs such as sweeping streets. They had to live away from other people, were not allowed in temples or to send children to schools attended by children of other groups. A law has given Untouchables the same rights as other people. But although the caste system has lost much of its power in the cities, it is still strong out in the countryside.

God (Brahma) is present in every thing and every place. People can find God by dedicating their work to him, by prayer (mantras) and love, by living alone and spending their days thinking about God. Until people find God, their souls keep on being born again and again (reincarnation) and in each life they are rewarded or punished for what they have done in the previous life (karma). When people find God, their souls are merged in God and they are not born again.

Hindu women are more likely than Muslim women to wear the bindi (red dot between eyebrows).

Hindus celebrate many festivals. Divali is New Year between late October and mid-November. It is the Festival of Lights because small earthernware lamps are lit inside and outside houses. Lamps are often floated along rivers. Presents are given and Lakshmi visits every house lit by a lamp.

Most Hindu homes have a shrine for offerings and prayers. It can be a room, small altar, picture or statue.

## Write down the Hindu names for the following.

a) main god _____

b) prayer _____

c) rebirth of souls _____

d) reward and punishment _____

e) life-preserving god _____

f) god the destroyer _____

g) Untouchables _____

h) goddess of learning _____

i) sacred river _____

j) Festival of Lights _____

k) holy city _____

l) facial red dot _____

m) goddess of wealth _____

n) sacred snake _____

o) remover of obstacles god _____

## How much do you know already? page 2
**1** a) North America, b) South America, c) Europe, d) Africa, e) Antarctica, f) Australia, g) Asia
**2** blue = any area around NZ, green = where E is, yellow = between NZ and Australia, red = above Europe
**3** 1 USA, 2 Canada, 3 Jamaica, 4 Honduras, 5 Colombia, 6 Peru, 7 Bolivia, 8 Argentina, 9 South Africa, 10 Zimbabwe, 11 Sierra Leone, 12 Egypt, 13 Great Britain, 14 France, 15 Germany, 16 Italy, 17 Greece, 18 Israel, 19 Iraq, 20 Saudi Arabia, 21 Afghanistan, 22 Russia, 23 India, 24 China, 25 Myanmar, 26 Malaysia, 27 Singapore, 28 Indonesia, 29 Papua New Guinea, 30 Japan, 31 Solomon Islands, 32 Tonga
**4** A Balkans, B Middle East, C Indochina, D Monsoon Asia, E Oceania, F Bermuda Triangle, G Sunshine Coast
**5** a) Australia, b) Iraq, c) Africa, d) USA, e) Japan, f) see p. 5 for position of equator line, g) USA, h) Russia, i) Israel, j) Greece, k) India

## Australasia page 4
desert = Oz, cane toad = Oz, mountains = NZ, earthquakes = NZ, volcanoes = NZ, Union Jack = Oz, NZ, pavlova = Oz, NZ, democracy = Oz, NZ, dingo = Oz, Asians = Oz, NZ, English = Oz, NZ, Tasman = Oz, NZ

## Indochina page 8
**1** a) Laos/Vientiane, b) Kampuchea/Phnom Penh, c) Vietnam/Hanoi
**2** tigers, snakes, heat, jungle, opium, rice, bears, panthers, communism

## Middle East page 9
**1** a) Abu Dhabi, b) Palestinian Authority, c) Egypt, d) water, e) Palestinians and Kurds

## United Kingdom of Great Britain (UK) page 10
**2** Philip in top box, Anne in second to left bottom box, William in first line under box containing Charles, Henry in second line under box containing Charles, Andrew in third to left bottom box

## Ireland and Northern Ireland page 11
**3** a) Protestant, b) Catholic, c) Catholic, d) Protestant, e) Catholic, f) Catholic

## The Balkans page 12
**1** red = Albania, Bosnia and Herzegovina, Croatia, Bulgaria, Greece, Macedonia, Moldova, Romania, Serbia, Montenegro
**2** Austria ✗, Romania ✓, Slovenia ✗, Francis Ferdinand ✗, Italy ✗, NATO ✗, Bulgaria ✗, Sarajevo ✓, Kosovo ✓, Bosnia ✓, Albania ✓, Turkish Empire ✗

## Russia and the old USSR page 13
**2** a) Stalin, b) Warsaw Pact, c) Chechens, d) Kursk, e) Kruschchev, f) USSR

**3** any order: Finland, Estonia, Latvia, Belarus, Ukraine, Georgia, Kazakstan, Mongolia, China

## Africa page 14
**1** a) Europe, b) Mediterranean Sea and Red Sea c) Suez Canal, d) Arabian Peninsula, e) tropic of Cancer, equator, tropic of Capricorn, f) Sahara Desert and Kalihari Desert, g) Congo Basin h) Madagascar, i) Atlantic Ocean and Indian Ocean
**2** 305
**3** a case can be made to include others in political, agricultural and health, but these are the main ones: a) 6, 10, 11, 14, 15, 17, b) 3, 4, 5, 9, 13, 16; c) 8, 12, 18

## Kiwis on OE page 16
**1** 1 India, 2 South Africa, 3 Italy, 4 Argentina/Brazil, 5 Nepal, 6 Netherlands, 7 Spain, 8 UK, 9 Germany, 10 US, 11 Greece, 12 Scotland, 13 China, 14 Easter Island, 15 Australia, 16 Morocco, 17 France, 18 Japan, 19 Egypt, 20 Australia, 21 Australia, 22 Rwanda, 23 Canada, 24 Turkey, 25 Brazil, 26 Russia, 27 San Francisco US, 28 New York US, 29 Norway, 30 Canada/US
**2** In Australia = 15 (inland), 20 (top coast), 21 (bottom coast); in Pacific Ocean to east of NZ = 14; in Africa = 2 (bottom), 16 (top left), 19 (top right), 22 (middle); in South America = 4 (bottom), 25 (top); in North America = 10 (bottom middle), 23 (top), 27 (left middle), 28 (bottom right), 30 (top right); in Asia = 1 (bottom middle), 5 (above 1), 13 (middle near right), 18 (middle far right), 24 (middle left), 26 (top left); in Europe = 3 (bottom 2nd from left), 6 (opposite UK island), 7 (bottom far left), 8 (bottom UK island), 9 (above 3), 11 (bottom 3rd from left), 12 (top UK island), 17 (under 6), 29 (top)

## Developing and developed worlds page 18
**1** any order: Third World, South, non-industrialised, developing
**2** any order: North, industrialised, developed, West
**3** red = Somalia, Nepal, Haiti, Gambia, Afghanistan, Ethiopia, Honduras, Tonga; blue = Australia, Canada, NZ, Finland, Germany, France, Argentina
**4** growing their food, making their goods, borrowing money from them and having to pay back with interest, giving them cheap holiday destinations, providing cheap labour

## Different governments page 20
**1** a) Westminster, London, b) Beehive, Wellington, c) Kremlin, Moscow, d) Pentagon, Washington, e) White House, Washington
**2** a) communist, b) democracy, c) theocracy

## Different names for parliaments and leaders page 21
a) Sultan, b) Czar, c) House of Representatives,

d) tyrant, e) Parliament, f) National Assembly,
g) Senate, House of Representatives, h) dictator,
i) President

## Commonwealth of Nations  page 22
1 any order: Nigeria, Fiji, Pakistan, Zimbabwe
2 a) Mozambique, b) Commonwealth Day, c) British
Empire, d) CHOGM, e) Commonwealth Games,
f) monarchist, g) republican, h) Secretary-General

## United Nations (UN)  page 23
1 a) arrow to outer part of logo, b) arrow to solid
shapes in middle of logo, c) arrow to circle shape
2 a) New York, b) The Hague in Netherlands,
c) Geneva, Switzerland
3 a) United Nations, b) Food and Agriculture
Organisation, c) World Health Organisation,
d) UN Children's Fund, e) International Atomic
Energy Agency, f) UN Educational, Scientific and
Cultural Organisation
4 UNICEF

## Human rights and Amnesty International (AI)
page 24
3 a) pressure, b) commute, c) amnesty, d) right,
e) violate, f) declaration, g) universal,
h) international, i) abuse, j) conscience

## Clubs for countries  page 26
1 a) Asia Pacific Economic Cooperation ✓,
b) Association of Southeast Asian Nations ✗,
c) Australian New Zealand Closer Economic
Relations Trade Agreement ✓, d) European Union ✗,
e) Group of 77 ✗, f) Group of 8 ✗, g) North Atlantic
Treaty Organisation ✗, h) International Monetary
Fund ✓, i) Organisation for Economic Cooperation
and Development ✓
2 a) ANZUS, b) Australia, NZ, US, c) NZ, d) NZ is
nuclear free

## Buddhism  page 28
2 calmness, kindness, wisdom, tolerance, positive,
understanding, friendliness, karma, peace, nirvana

## Christianity  page 29
1 a) 5, b) 6, c) 2, d) 1, e) 3, f) 4
2 Presbyterianism, Anglicanism, Methodism, Roman
Catholicism, Baptist

## Hinduism  page 30
a) Brahma, b) mantra, c) reincarnation, d) karma,
e) Vishnu, f) Shiva g) Dalit, h) Saraswati, i) Ganges,
j) Diwali, k) Varanasi, l) bindi m) Lakshmi n) cobra,
o) Ganesha

## Islam  page 31
a) hajj = holy pilgrimage to Mecca, b) Iraq = Muslim
country, c) Islam = religion of Muslims, d) Allah =
the one God, e) Koran = holy book, f) Mecca = holy
city, g) jihad = struggle, holy war, h) Arabs = group
of people, not all are Muslims, i) Moses = figure
mentioned in Old Testament and Koran, j) Yemen =
Muslim country, k) Muslim = name for believers in

Islam, l) Moslem = name for believers in Islam,
m) Friday = Muslim holy day, n) mosque = church,
o) fatwah = killing for offending Islam, p) Ramadan
= holy month of fasting

## Judaism  page 32
1 a) Star of David, b) tallit, c) menorah, d) yarmulk
or bar mitzvah, e) rabbi
2 a) bat, b) bar, c) Wailing Wall, d) Star of David

## Sikhism  page 33
a) karma = destiny, as you sow, so you reap, b) Granth
= sacred book, c) gurdwara = church, d) Punjab =
Indian province, e) Sanskrit = extinct language,
f) guru = teacher, g) Nanak = Sikhism founder,
h) kesha = hair uncut under turban, i) kangha = comb,
j) kaccha = military shorts, k) kara = iron bracelet,
l) kirpan = dagger, m) turban = wrap for hair

## Arbor Day  page 34
1 a) pohutukawa, b) gum
2 shelter, shade, beauty; Latin, tree, arbor;
Nebraska; 1872, Morton; helmets, shampoo, tyres;
Israel, Japan, Iceland

## Saint Patrick's Day  page 35
1 colours of the rainbow = red, orange, yellow,
green, blue, indigo, violet
2 St Patrick gathered up all the snakes of Ireland,
put them in a box, and threw the box into the Irish
Sea

## Mother's Day and Father's Day  page 36
1 They honour people who have been like a mother
and father (OR father and mother) to you.
2 Rhea, Mothering Sunday, Ana Jarvis, President
Wilson, Sonora Dodd, President Coolidge, President
Johnson

## Valentine's Day  page 37
1 57
2 a) Cupid, b) Lupercalia, c) Romulus and Remus,
d) Romulus, e) Lupercal, f) Claudius 11, g) bow and
arrows, h) Valentine

## Guy Fawkes  page 38
1 a) treason, b) Protestant, c) King, d) barrels,
e) anonymous letter, f) nobles, g) England
2 the torch

## Halloween  page 39
Cross out: a) July 1, b) modern, c) unholy, d) day,
e) dog, f) All Turnips Day, g) US, h) water,
i) Nativity, j) Yuletide, k) Greek, l) rabbis,
m) oranges, n) whip, o) Lent, p) fungi, q) troll,
r) devil biscuits

## Changing names of places, people, animals  page 40
a) Thailand, b) Botswana, c) Kampuchea, d) Germany,
e) Ho Chi Minh City f) Myanmar, g) Beijing,
h) Ethiopia, i) Iran, j) Taiwan, k) Sri Lanka,
l) Bangladesh, m) Vanuatu, n) Chennai, o) Benin,
p) Tuvalu, q) Democratic Republic of the Congo,

r) Zimbabwe, s) Istanbul, t) Kolkata, u) Zambia
v) Yangoon, w) Mumbai, x) St Petersburg

## Globalisation   page 41
1 global village
2 any order: greater choice of goods to buy, living standards go up, more people travel overseas, more information is swapped, better understanding of other cultures, helps spread the idea of democracy, spreads technology around world
3 any order: increases materialism, developed countries do well but developing countries do badly, workers lose jobs, popular culture threaten to take over other cultures, huge companies are becoming more powerful and wealthy than some governments, companies wreck the environment

## GE/GM   page 42
2 DNA/genes, genea/kind, Dolly/clone, Monsanto/company, GE/GM, engineering/modification, DDT/asbestos, herbicides/pesticides

## Aids, Foot-and-mouth Disease, Mad Cow Disease   page 43
2 circle each group
3 x = unsafe sex, sharing drug needles

## Weapons of mass destruction   page 44
a) nerve, blister, choking, b) protective, c) mass, d) cobra, e) high, f) Desert, g) chemical, biological, germ, h) Peloponnesian, Gulf, World, i) mustard, tear, chlorine, j) concentration, k) bubonic, l) robot, m) huge, n) plague, o) toxic p) miniature

## Terrorism   page 45
1 c
2 a) US, b) Indonesia, c) US, d) Israel, e) Afghanistan

## Drug trafficking   page 46
a) Southeast Asia, b) opium poppy, c) morphine, d) Myanmar e) trafficking, f) Bangkok, g) east, h) US, i) China (Kunming and Guangzhou), j) Hong Kong, Taiwan

## Refugees   page 47
1 a) Lebanon, Syria, Jordan, Egypt, West Bank, Gaza Strip, b) Gaza Strip, West Bank, c) Israel
2 a) 7, b) 4, c) 3, d) 5, e) 6, f) 2, g) 1

## Extreme natural events   page 48
1 a) tsunami, b) lightning, c) fire
2 a) earthquake, b) tornado, c) snowstorm, d) tsunami, e) fire, f) volcano, g) tropical cyclone, h) flood, i) heat wave

## El Nino   page 49
2 a) The Little Boy or Christ Child, b) seven, c) 36, d) Pacific, e) La Nina, The Little Girl, f) drought, floods, g) normal, world h) eastern, Pacific

## Ozone hole   page 50
Across: 1 more, 5 tropics, 6 loss, 7 not, 9 web, 10 hole, 13 antarctic, 16 sun, 18 gas, 19 skin
Down: 2 ozone, 3 South, 4 used, 8 blocks, 9 wraps, 11 drift, 12 thin, 14 takes, 15 thick, 17 UV

## Endangered rainforest and species   page 51
2 Any order: slashing and burning to make farms and ranches, mining, cutting trees for logs, destroying homes for plants and animals, capturing animals for pets

## Kyoto Agreement   page 52
1 US, China, Russia, Japan, India, Germany, Britain, Canada, South Korea, Ukraine
2 In order clockwise = nitrous oxide 6%, $CO_2$ 54%, CFCs 21%, methane 12%, ozone 7%
3 a) million metric tonnes, b) sending or letting out, c) 1800, 2000

## The Bermuda Triangle   page 53
1 a) Miami = far left, Bermuda = far right, Puerto Rico = bottom
2 a) triangle, b) Triangle, c) Sea, d) disappearances, e) disappearances, f) compass, g) north, h) navigation, i) Stream, j) storms, k) spouts, l) floor

## Space   page 54
a) *Apollo 11* moon landing, b) Hubble telescope, c) US space shuttle *Challenger* exploded, d) US space shuttle *Columbia* broke up, e) building International Space Station, f) *Sputnik 1* launched, g) 1966 Treaty

## Olympic Games   page 55
1 left to right; top = blue, black, red; bottom = yellow, green
2 Any order: stadium, Olympia, wrestling, pentathlon, equestrian, taekwondo, bobsleigh, Coubertin, solidarity, archery, citius, contestants

## Obesity   page 56
1 overweight = 4 underweight = 1, obese = 3, average weight = 2
2 any order: less physical activity, food is more easily available, less physical leisure activities, 'junk food', massive advertising for 'junk food'
3 breathing problems, musculo-skeletal problems, skin problems, infertility, diabetes, gall bladder disease, high blood pressure, stroke, coronary heart disease, parents outliving children

## Life expectancy   page 57
1 a) x, b) ✓, c) x, d) x, e) ✓, f) x, g) ✓, h) ✓, i) x, j) x
2 a) mortality, b) morbidity, c) disability, d) nutrition, e) sanitation, f) hygiene, g) life expectancy

## Examples of inspirational people   page 58
a) Princess Diana, b) American flag, c) Ground Zero, d) apartheid, e) Calcutta, f) China, g) India

## Final challenge    page 59

1 turnip
2 Allah
3 Hanoi
4 Mediterranean Sea
5 Pacific
6 greenhouse gases
7 yarmulk
8 bulimia
9 many islands
10 five
11 obesity
12 Indonesia
13 submarine
14 Lenin
15 civil
16 Iraq
17 India
18 Russia
19 El Nino
20 Catholic
21 sheep
22 Iraq
23 volcano
24 morphine
25 Israel
26 Sri Lanka
27 monarchist
28 theocracy
29 nirvana
30 Bonn
31 Australia and NZ
32 Mediterranean
33 NZ
34 humans
35 al Qaeda
36 India
37 5
38 desert
39 Cupid
40 Edinburgh
41 Divali
42 Islam
43 Republic of Ireland
44 1948
45 Frenchman
46 anti-semitism
47 stratosphere
48 St Patrick
49 2001
50 Sikh temple

51 communist
52 shamrock
53 dictator
54 Russia
55 emir
56 earthquake
57 OECD
58 hallow
59 Moscow
60 The One Who Knows
61 Inuit
62 Hoodoo Sea
63 Thailand
64 World War 2
65 The North
66 Commonwealth
67 Christians
68 virus
69 tree
70 Australia
71 Sarejevo
72 Asia Pacific
73 Yugoslavia
74 Belfast
75 14 February
76 Switzerland
77 Iraq
78 Madagascar
79 Palestinian uprising
80 South Pole
81 The Destroyer
82 plain
83 Judaism
84 Koran
85 Kurds
86 astronautics
87 Damascus
88 Iraq
89 Protestantism
90 Windsor
91 South Africa
92 Saudi Arabia
93 Dalit
94 Vietnam
95 India
96 the same thing
97 Amnesty International
98 London
99 Cambodia
100 7

Islam:
- is the name for the religion of Muslims (Moslems)
- is the fastest growing religion in the world (of every four people, one is Muslim)
- in Arabic means 'submission to God'
- began in Arabia but not all Arabs are Muslims
- is a main religion in Algeria, Bahrain, Bangladesh, Benin, Brunei, Cameroon, Comoros, Djibouti, Egypt, Gabon, Gambia, Indonesia, Iran, Iraq, Kuwait, Lebanon, Libya, Maldives, Morocco, Mozambique, Nigeria, Oman, Pakistan, Qatar, Saudi Arabia, Senegal, Somalia, Sudan, Syria, Tunisia, Yemen, Turkey.

## LINKS TO CHRISTIANS AND JEWS

- Muslims believe in only one God. Muslims call this God Allah. In Arabic it means 'the God'.
- Adam, Noah, Abraham, Ishmael, Moses and David (from the Bible's Old Testament) are all mentioned in the Koran.
- Like Christians and Jews, Muslims regard Jerusalem as a holy city. (Two other holy cities for Muslims are in Saudi Arabia – Mecca and Medina.)
- Muslims have the story of Jesus Christ in their holy book but they regard Jesus as a prophet, not as the Son of God. Muslims believe that the greatest and last of the prophets was Mohammed (Muhammad, Muhammed), c 570-632.

## OTHER CUSTOMS

- Alcohol is banned.
- Friday is the Muslim holy day.
- Jihad is a struggle and striving eg to be a better person. This is sometimes interpreted as a holy war.
- A fatwah is a religious decree or ruling on a point of Islamic law by a recognised authority such as a Mufti, Judge or Scholar. For example, when a young female wrote an article about the Miss World competition in 2002 and said Mohammed would have approved of it, Islam declared a fatwah on her.

## THE KORAN

The Muslim holy book (Koran or Quran) gives information about how Muslims should live, dress and behave. It says they must do five main things:
1  recite the creed which says *'There is no god but Allah; and Mohammed is the apostle of God'*
2  pray five times a day though not necessarily in a mosque (church)
3  give alms (gifts of money) to help the poor
4  fast during the month of Ramadan (no eating or drinking between sunrise and sunset)
5  make a pilgrimage (journey called a hajj) to Mecca once in a lifetime.

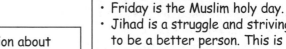

Write in the missing letters to make a word important to Islam and then write in the meaning of the word.

| WORD | MEANING | WORD | MEANING |
|---|---|---|---|
| a) H – J J | | i) M – S – S | |
| b) – R – Q | | j) Y – M – N | |
| c) – S L – M | | k) M – S L – M | |
| d) – L L – H | | l) M – S L – M | |
| e) K – R – N | | m) F R – D – Y | |
| f) M – C C – | | n) M – S Q – – | |
| g) J – H – D | | o) F – T W – H | |
| h) – R – B S | | p) R – M – D – N | |

# JUDAISM

## BELIEFS

Judaism is the religion of Jews
There is only one God
God created all things
God is the source of all Righteousness
The Old Testament (but not the New Testament)
The Messiah (Deliverer) will come one day
Jesus Christ was not the Messiah

## FAMOUS FIGURES IN JEWISH HISTORY

**Abraham** (Jews trace history back to him)
**Isaac** (Abraham's son)
**Jacob** (Abraham's grandson, aka Israel)
**Moses** (received the 10 Commandments)
**Saul** (first king)
**David** (second king, made Jerusalem his capital)
**Solomon** (third king, built temple in Jerusalem)

## SYMBOLS

**chuppah** – canopy used in marriage celebration
**Hebrew** – language of the Torah
**kosher** – food prepared under strict rules
**menorah** – nine-branched candelabrum
**rabbi** – master teacher
**Sabbath** – Friday evening till Saturday evening
**Star of David** – symbol of Jewry
**synagogue** – Jewish church
**tallit** – shawl worn during services
**Talmud** – oral tradition interpreting the Torah
**Torah** – sacred law and teachings
**Wailing Wall** – place of prayer in Jerusalem
**yarmulk** – skullcap worn during prayers

## ISRAEL

Jews have a long history with the land known as *The Holy Land, Palestine, The Promised Land*. This is roughly the place where the country of Israel is today. Jews proclaimed the new country of Israel as a Jewish state in 1948. It was in the middle of Arab countries, which were largely Muslim. Throughout history, Jews were often forced to live away from the Holy Land. They call this the diaspora. The new country of Israel said any Jew from any part of the world was welcome to come and live in Israel.

## ANTI-SEMITISM (HATRED OF JEWS)

Jews have been persecuted in many times and in many countries. Some reasons are:
- they were blamed for the crucifixion of Jesus Christ
- they practised usury (lending of money for a profit)
- they made an easy scapegoat for non-Jews to blame when things went wrong such as plagues
- they were made to wear clothes such as yellow hats to show they were Jews; this made them different
- they were made to live in special areas called ghettos and this made them different

## FESTIVALS

Rosh Hashanah – New Year
Yom Kippur – Day of Atonement
Pesach – Passover
Hannukah – Chanukah, Festival of Lights
bar mitzvah – coming-of-age for 13-year-old boy
bat mitzvah – coming-of-age for 12-year-old girl

---

**1** Write in each box what is being shown in the picture.

 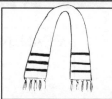   

a) _____  b) _____  c) _____  d) _____  e) _____

**2** Detective work.

a)  The most likely word for 'girl' is _____
b)  The most likely word for 'boy' is _____
c)  The most likely name for the remains of an ancient temple of Jerusalem that is also called the Western Wall is _____
d)  The most likely star on the flag of Israel is _____

# SIKHISM

Sikhism comes from a Sanskrit word 'Sikha' meaning 'disciple'. (Sanskrit is an extinct language.)

Sikhism developed in the late 15th century as an effort to bring Hindu and Muslim ideas closer together.

The idea that Sikhism is a form of Hinduism is wrong and offends Sikhs.

They believe in a single, invisible God. They also believe in the Hindu ideas of reincarnation and karma.

80% of Sikhs live in Punjab state in northwest India where the faith began.

Its founder was Guru Nanak. He was followed by nine other gurus (teachers). Nanak taught Sikhs could reach God by serving fellow humans, living a life of love, devotion, prayers and good deeds.

Place of worship is a gurdwara (temple).

The Sikh sacred book is called Granth.

Sikh men became famous as warriors. They are easy to pick out by the 5 Ks - **kesha** (hair worn uncut and knotted under a turban) **kangha** (comb) **kaccha** (military shorts) **kara** (iron bracelet) **kirpan** (short dagger).

Unravel these words, all important to Sikhism, and write short meanings for them.

a) A A K M R _____

b) A G H R N T _____

c) A A D G R R U W _____

d) A B J N P U _____

e) A I K N R S S T _____

f) G R U U _____

g) A A K N N _____

h) A E H K S _____

i) A A G H K N _____

j) A A C C H K _____

k) A A K R _____

l) A I K P N R _____

m) A B N R T U _____

# ARBOR DAY

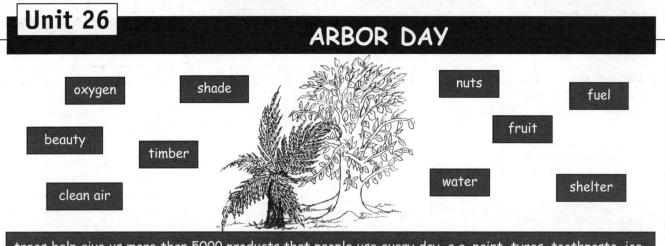

oxygen    shade    nuts    fuel

beauty    fruit

timber

clean air    water    shelter

trees help give us more than 5000 products that people use every day, e.g. paint, tyres, toothpaste, ice cream, <u>helmets</u>, chewing gum, milk shakes, toilet seats, nail polish, <u>movies</u>, rocket fuel, deodorants, fireworks, shampoo, cosmetics, dyes, piano keys, sausage casings

Where Arbor Day comes from:
- a man called Julius Sterling Morton and his wife went to live in Nebraska
- Julius was <u>used</u> to trees around him but Nebraska had hardly any
- Julius suggested people set aside <u>one</u> day of the year to plant <u>trees</u>
- first Arbor Day held in 1872 in Nebraska in <u>US</u>. Arbor is the Latin word for tree
- on that first Arbor Day, Nebraska people planted about one million trees

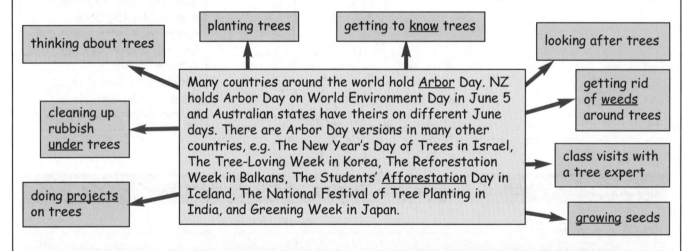

thinking about trees

planting trees

getting to <u>know</u> trees

looking after trees

cleaning up rubbish <u>under</u> trees

getting rid of <u>weeds</u> around trees

Many countries around the world hold <u>Arbor</u> Day. NZ holds Arbor Day on World Environment Day in June 5 and Australian states have theirs on different June days. There are Arbor Day versions in many other countries, e.g. The New Year's Day of Trees in Israel, The Tree-Loving Week in Korea, The Reforestation Week in Balkans, The Students' <u>Afforestation</u> Day in Iceland, The National Festival of Tree Planting in India, and Greening Week in Japan.

class visits with a tree expert

doing <u>projects</u> on trees

<u>growing</u> seeds

**1** Take the first letter of the underlined words and rearrange them to make the name of two famous trees you could plant on Arbor Day.

a) P _ _ _ _ _ _ _ _ _          b) G _ _

**2** Sort the words from the box into groups of three.

| shelter | Latin | Israel | Nebraska | tree | helmets | arbor | 1872 |
| Japan | shampoo | shade | tyres | beauty | Iceland | Morton | |

a) _____    _____    _____

b) _____    _____    _____

c) _____    _____    _____

d) _____    _____    _____

e) _____    _____    _____

## About Saint Patrick

**Date of birth:** about 389    **Given name:** Maewyn
**Place of birth:** possibly Wales    **Date of death:** 461
**Financial status of parents:** wealthy

**First visit to Ireland:** captured by pirates when he was 16 from his father's estate and taken to Ireland as a slave; escaped home after six years

**Second visit to Ireland:** had a dream telling him to convert Irish to Christianity so went back as a bishop (convert = to turn into)

**Work in Ireland:** bishop, preached Christianity

**Shamrock:** said to have used the three leaves of the shamrock plant to explain the Trinity of God – the Father, Son and Holy Ghost

**Legend:** he put all the snakes in Ireland into a box and threw it into the sea; this explains why there are no snakes there today and why the Irish Sea is so rough

**Possible truth about legend:** no snakes were native to Ireland so the legend could be a symbol for people converting to Christianity

**Status in Ireland today:** patron saint (patron = protector, supporter)

**Date of St Patrick's Day:** March 17 (anniversary of his death)

**Importance of St Patrick's Day:** known as the biggest celebration in the world; Irish everywhere dress in green and hold parades, speeches, feasts.

Popular symbols of Ireland
- shamrock – three-leaved clover
- rainbow – has a pot of gold at the end of it
- leprechaun – Irish fairy
- green – colour of spring and shamrock, symbol of hope and nature

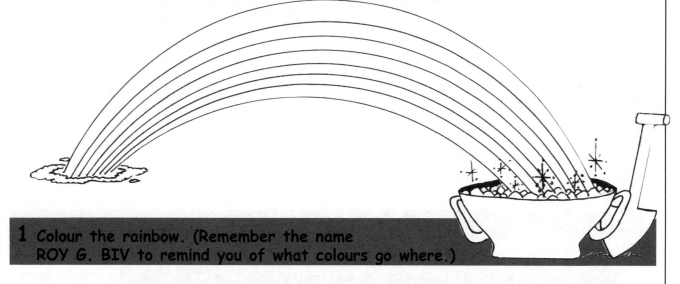

**1** Colour the rainbow. (Remember the name ROY G. BIV to remind you of what colours go where.)

**2** Write the snake legend inside the snake.

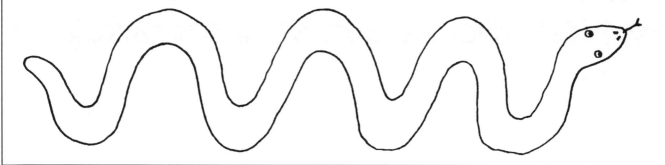

# MOTHER'S DAY AND FATHER'S DAY

You can celebrate these days even if you don't have a mother or a father because they are days to honour and remember anyone who has been like a mother or father to you.

## MOTHER'S DAY

Ancient Greeks celebrated a special day in honour of Rhea, the Mother of the Gods.

In the 1600s, England held a day called Mothering Sunday, to honour the mothers of England. It was celebrated on the fourth Sunday of Lent (the 40-day period leading up to Easter). At this time many poor people worked as servants for the rich. On Mothering Sunday the servants got the day off to go home to see their mothers. They took a special cake called the mothering cake. Later this day got mixed in with a celebration to honour the Mother Church.

In 1907 in the USA Ana Jarvis from Philadelphia began a campaign to set up a national Mother's Day. She persuaded her mother's church to celebrate Mother's Day on the anniversary of her mother's death. This was the second Sunday of May.

Ana and others began a letter-writing campaign to set up a national Mother's Day. In 1914, President Wilson set up a national Mother's Day for the second Sunday of May each year.

Today Mother's Day is celebrated in many different countries at different times, although many countries such as NZ, Australia, Denmark, Finland, Italy, Turkey and Belgium have theirs on the second Sunday in May.

## FATHER'S DAY

In 1909 Sonora Dodd of Washington wanted a special day to honour her father, William Smart. William had been a Civil War soldier who was widowed when his wife died in childbirth with their sixth child. He raised the children by himself on his farm.

The first Father's Day was observed in 1910 in Spokane, Washington.

In 1924 President Coolidge supported the idea of a national Father's Day, and made it the third Sunday in June.

In 1966 President Johnson signed a proclamation declaring the third Sunday of June as Father's Day. Other countries hold a Father's Day. NZ's is on the first Sunday of September.

---

**1** Rearrange the words in the box to make a sentence about Mother's Day and Father's Day.

have a father to people you. like mother They been and honour who

SENTENCE: _____

**2** Put in order of earliest to latest appearance in the story of both days.

Sonora Dodd, President Johnson, President Wilson, Ana Jarvis, Rhea, Mothering Sunday, President Coolidge

ORDER: _____

_____

Nobody knows exactly how Valentine's Day got its name. Some stories are:

[1] St Valentine was a Roman who refused to give up Christianity so he was put to death. He left a farewell note for the jailer's daughter who had become his friend. He signed the note *From your Valentine*. The daughter was blind but his prayers or note brought her sight back.

[2] Roman Emperor Claudius couldn't get soldiers to fight for him because they didn't want to leave their loved ones. So he cancelled all marriages in Rome. St Valentine was a priest in Rome. He secretly married couples. He was caught and put to death.

[3] It was connected with the Lupercalia, a February festival of ancient Rome in honour of Lupercus, a god. It was held in the Lupercal cave in Rome where legend said a wolf had once looked after two young boys, twins Romulus and Remus. Romulus is said to have later founded the city of Rome. Boys and girls were usually kept separate but for Lupercalia, the names of girls were put in a jar. Boys drew names out, and that boy and girl would be partners (valentines) for the festival.

Over time, 14 February became the date for swapping love messages and St Valentine became the special saint of lovers.

Cupid is a love symbol because he was the ancient Roman god of love. He was a naughty winged child. He would shoot arrows at people and cause them to fall in love.

> valentine = a sweetheart; or a card or gift sent by one person to another on Valentine's Day (14 February)

> Later the custom was to wear the names of your partner on your sleeve. This is where today's expression of wearing your heart on your sleeve (meaning you let the world see who your girlfriend or boyfriend is) comes from.

**1** Count the number of hearts you can find on the page. _____

**2** Write down names for the following.

a) Roman god of love _____

b) an ancient Roman festival _____

c) twin brothers of legend _____

d) legendary founder of Rome _____

e) a Roman cave _____

f) a cruel Emperor _____

g) what the god of love carried _____

h) a legendary saint _____

# GUY FAWKES

"I'm King James I. Some of my nobles are Catholics. But I'm not Catholic, I'm Protestant. And that's that. This is therefore a Protestant kingdom."

"We're all Catholic. And the only way we'll get a better deal for Catholics in this country is to start an uprising against that Protestant king of ours and his Parliament."

"We'll blow up Parliament on the day James opens it. That's the 5th of November."

"We'll hire a cellar under the House of Lords and then we'll put barrels of gunpowder down there."

"36 barrels of gunpowder should do the job. We'll blow the place sky-high."

"I know just the man we need. Guy Fawkes. He's a soldier and he's very brave. He can pretend to be a servant so he can go to and fro from the cellar. He can arrange the gunpowder down there. On the day, he can light the fuse and escape."

"Nobody's suspected a thing. I'll cover these barrels with firewood and coal."

GUN POWDER

"Someone's sent me an anonymous letter. It's warning me to stay away from the opening of Parliament."

"Something's fishy. I smell a plot."

"Let's search the cellars."

"Ha ha, what have we here? Caught in the act. Getting ready to light the gunpowder, were you?"

"I think this country will remember this day for a long time. This is the day Parliament and king just missed being blown up."

"I sentence you, Guy Fawkes, and the other seven plotters, to death for treason."

JUDGE

"Remember, remember, the fifth of November, Gunpowder, treason and plot, We know no reason, why gunpowder treason Should ever be forgot"

## 1 Write down the words for the following.

a) being disloyal and plotting against your country _____

b) the religion in England in 1605 that was non-Catholic _____

c) the job that James I held _____

d) what the gunpowder in the cellar was packed in _____

e) an unsigned letter _____

f) people with a lot of power who associated with the king _____

g) the country that gave the idea of Guy Fawkes Day to many others

## 2 Write down the one thing in the cartoon strip that is out of place for 1605.

_____

# HALLOWEEN

Halloween is one of the oldest holidays in the world. It is a mix of:

- an ancient Celtic festival called Samhain. Celts lived in Great Britain and Northern France. On 31 October they put out their cooking fires while their priests, known as druids, lit new fires on a hill and offered sacrifices of crops and animals. They danced round the fire to keep spirits away and next day gave an ember from the fire to each family to start new cooking fires.
- a Pomona festival, which celebrated fruits, especially apples, that the Romans brought when they invaded Britain.
- All Saints Day (called Hallowmas) to honour the saints, and All Souls Day to honour the dead, started by the Roman Catholic church.

Parts of all these festivals got joined together in what is now Halloween.

31 October = Halloween. Hallow (old word) = holy. E'en = Scottish for evening. It was taken to the US from Europe and is today celebrated in many countries all around the world.

A legend said a man named Jack was so wicked that when he died he was not let into Heaven or Hell. The devil gave him an ember in a hollowed-out turnip to light his way through the darkness. Celts carried these lanterns – embers in big turnips – on the eve of 31 October to keep evil spirits away. When the custom was taken to the US, the jack-o-lantern became a hollowed-out pumpkin because there were more pumpkins than turnips in the US.

On All Souls Day, people walked from village to village begging for soul cakes. In return for cakes they promised to say a prayer for the dead to help them get into Heaven. Over time, it became the children who did the begging. This became the custom of trick or treating.

Young people put nuts on the hearth to see if their sweethearts were true to them. If the nut burned normally all was well but if the nut cracked the sweetheart was untrue. Another game was bobbing (catching in the mouth) apples floating in a tub of water.

To see a witch you had to put clothes on inside out and walk backwards on Halloween. People thought witches could change into cats.

## Cross out the wrong alternatives about Halloween.

a)  1 July/31 October

b)  old/modern

c)  holy/unholy

d)  evening/day

e)  dog/cat

f)  All Souls Day/All Turnips Day

g)  worldwide/US

h)  water/fire

i)  Nativity/Samhain

j)  Pomona/Yuletide

k)  Greek/Celtic

l)  druids/rabbis

m) oranges/apples

n)  whip/ember

o)  Hallowmas/Lent

p)  fungi/nuts

q)  witch/troll

r)  soul cakes/devil biscuits

# CHANGING NAMES OF PEOPLE, PLACES, ANIMALS

**Some places are called different names by different people**

e.g. Mt Everest
English call it *Everest*
Tibetans call it *Chomolungma*
Chinese call it *Qomolangma*
Nepalese call it *Sagarmatha*

**Sometimes countries break up into two or more other countries**

e.g. Yugoslavia is now Bosnia and Herzegovina, Croatia, Macedonia, Montenegro, Serbia, Slovenia

**Sometimes two countries join to become one**

e.g. East and West Germany are now Germany

**Sometimes countries shift their capitals**

e.g. the German capital has moved from Bonn to Berlin

**Sometimes places are given names by Europeans when they first see the places and later, the places get back their native names**

e.g. Ayers Rock/Uluru in Australia and Mt Egmont/Taranaki in NZ

**Sometimes a group gets a new (or old) name**

e.g. Eskimos are now better known as *Inuit*

**Sometimes new places are created**

e.g. Nunavut is a new territory of Canada set up for Inuit

**Sometimes countries change their names**

e.g. *Abyssinia* is now **Ethiopia**
*Burma* is now **Myanmar**
*Bechuanaland* is now **Botswana**
*Cambodia* is now also its local name of **Kampuchea**
*Ceylon* is now **Sri Lanka**
*Dahomey* is now **Benin**
*East Pakistan* is now **Bangladesh**
*Ellice Islands* is now **Tuvalu**
*Formosa* is now **Taiwan**
*Gilbert, Line* and *Phoenix Is* is now **Kiribati**
*New Hebrides* is now **Vanuatu**
*Northern Rhodesia* is now **Zambia**
*Persia* is now **Iran**
*Portuguese East Africa* is now **Mozambique**
*Rhodesia* (Southern Rhodesia) is now **Zimbabwe**
*Siam* is now **Thailand**
*Western Samoa* is now **Samoa**
*Zaire* is now **Democratic Republic of the Congo**

**Sometimes animals get a name change**

e.g. NZ's North Island Hector's dolphin is now called Maui's dolphin

**Sometimes cities change their names**

e.g. *Benares* is now **Varanasi**
*Bombay* is now **Mumbai**
*Calcutta* is now **Kolkata**
*Constantinople* is now **Istanbul**
*Leningrad* is now **St Petersburg**
*Madras* is now **Chennai**
*Peking* is now **Beijing**
*Rangoon* is now **Yangoon**
*Saigon* is now **Ho Chi Minh City**

---

**The wrong list of names has been used. In the boxes, write the modern names.**

| Siam | Bechuanaland | Cambodia | East Germany | Saigon |
|---|---|---|---|---|
| a) | b) | c) | d) | e) |

| Burma | Peking | Abyssinia | Persia | Formosa |
|---|---|---|---|---|
| f) | g) | h) | i) | j) |

| Ceylon | East Pakistan | New Hebrides | Madras | Dahomey |
|---|---|---|---|---|
| k) | l) | m) | n) | o) |

| Ellice Island | Zaire | S. Rhodesia | Constantinople | Calcutta |
|---|---|---|---|---|
| p) | q) | r) | s) | t) |

| Northern Rhodesia | Rangoon | Bombay | Leningrad |
|---|---|---|---|
| u) | v) | w) | x) |

# GLOBALISATION

The term 'globalisation' was first used in the 1980s but the idea is older.

**What globalisation means:**
- the transfer of goods, information and ideas among countries.
- goods, information and ideas can now travel the world quickly, easily, cheaply.
- goods, information and ideas are going everywhere at the same time.
- the world is becoming a global village linked together by the Internet and telecommunications.
- every person in the world is getting joined into a single world society.
- the world is becoming a global shopping mall.
- the world is shrinking.

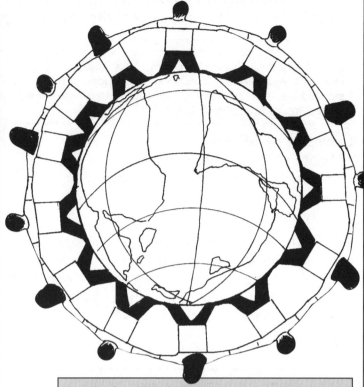

**People against globalisation say:**
- it increases materialism (people wanting to buy goods they don't necessarily need).
- developed countries do well but developing countries do badly.
- workers, especially manual labourers, in developed countries lose out when companies shift production overseas where labour is cheaper.
- popular culture such as Hollywood and McDonald's threaten to take over other cultures in other countries.
- huge companies are becoming more powerful and wealthy than some governments.
- companies wreck the environment because all they are interested in is money.

**People for globalisation say:**
- people have greater choice of goods to buy.
- living standards go up.
- more people travel overseas.
- more information is swapped.
- better understanding of other cultures.
- helps spread the idea of democracy.
- spreads technology around the world.

**1** In the box on each back above, write a letter that helps make up a description for globalisation. (Clue: check out terms in 'What globalisation means'.)

**2** Write down four possible good points about globalisation.

a) _____

b) _____

c) _____

d) _____

**3** Write down four possible bad points about globalisation.

a) _____

b) _____

c) _____

d) _____

# GE/GM

GE = genetic engineering
GM = genetic modification

GE and GM are the same thing. They mean changing genes so that something from one organism (plants and animals are called organisms) can be put into another organism.

Every living organism has DNA. (Find the DNA pic on the cover of this book.) DNA is *very* small. You can't see it with your naked eye. DNA has genes. Humans have about 3 billion genes. Genes decide things such as what colour skin and eyes you have. Genetic means all about genes. The old Greek word "genea" means "a kind" or "a breed".

Examples of GE/GM:
* bacteria genes into corn
* manmade toad genes into potatoes
* human genes into pigs
* jellyfish genes into mice.

GE/GM is controversial. Some people say things such as growing a human ear on the back of a mouse is too weird, and we'll soon be eating Frankenstein-food. Other people say organisms such as Dolly, the cloned sheep, are the way the future should be going.

For example:

| ARGUMENTS FOR GE/GM CROPS | ARGUMENTS AGAINST GE/GM CROPS |
|---|---|
| • bigger crops means less land needed<br>• new medicines developed<br>• starvation in the world stopped<br>• fewer pesticides, herbicides, fertilisers<br>• less chemicals better for people and environment<br>• drought- and cold-resistant plants<br>• disease- and weed-resistant plants<br>• food looks better<br>• food stores longer on shelves<br>• food tastes better<br>• removal of allergic substances in food will help allergic people<br>• more healthy food, e.g. potatoes that absorb less fat when fried | • not been proved safe<br>• 'safe' things from history such as asbestos and DDT were later found to be unsafe<br>• once GE is started you can't go back<br>• new poisons and diseases could appear<br>• new weed-resistant plants could get out of control<br>• new crops could harm environment<br>• GE in one plant could escape into other plants<br>• might create new allergens in food<br>• huge power that GM companies could get, e.g. Monsanto American company behind many GM crops<br>• interferes with nature |

## 1 Find the following words in this unit and underline them.

asbestos    clone    company    DDT    DNA    Dolly    engineering    GE    genea
genes    GM    herbicides    kind    modification    Monsanto    pesticides

## 2 Sort the words in the list above into sensible pairs.

_____/_____    _____/_____

_____/_____    _____/_____

_____/_____    _____/_____

_____/_____    _____/_____

## HIV = Human Immunodeficiency Virus, AIDS = Acquired Immune Deficiency Syndrome

- if you are infected with HIV, you are said to have AIDS when the HIV has weakened your immune system so much you can't fight off other illnesses
- there are tiny amounts of HIV in saliva, tears, blisters; there is none in urine, faeces, vomit, sweat; there are infectious amounts in blood, blood products, body fluids
- HIV is not carried by air, water, food, mosquitoes (they don't inject blood from other people they've bitten)
- HIV does not survive very long outside the human body
- HIV is passed by unprotected sex, injection gear or transfusion of contaminated blood, skin grafts and organ transplants from infected people. It is also passed from infected mothers to their babies (pregnancy, birth or breast-feeding).
- HIV/AIDS hits every country, race, age group
- many people can't afford the expensive drugs to slow AIDS down
- people living with HIV/AIDS = millions; total AIDS deaths over the years = millions; total AIDS deaths of children over the years = millions; total AIDS orphans over the years = millions; people newly infected with HIV this year = millions; AIDS deaths this year = millions

DISEASE

## SARS = Severe Acute Respiratory Syndrome (caused by a virus)

- burst onto the world scene at the end of 2002
- began in China and as infected people travelled, SARS began infecting and killing other people worldwide
- measures to stop the spread of SARS included the wearing of masks, putting people in quarantine, banning wakes for victims, sealing off hospitals, travel warnings to avoid places where infection rates were high.

## Foot-and-mouth disease

- causes fever and blisters, mainly on mouths and feet
- affects cattle, sheep, pigs, goats
- can spread rapidly, and is very infectious
- can even be picked up and carried by the wheels of vehicles on roads
- people can spread it but they rarely catch it
- wastes animals and this is why farmers fear it and governments order mass killings of infected animals

## 1 Colour in (red) the World AIDS Awareness ribbon.

## 2 Circle the groups affected by HIV/AIDS.

| men | women | youth | children | babies |

## 3 Cross the boxes which are beside high risk activities for getting HIV.

- ☐ unsafe sex
- ☐ sharing cutlery
- ☐ shaking hands
- ☐ using swimming pools
- ☐ using public toilets
- ☐ sharing drug needles
- ☐ kissing
- ☐ sneezing
- ☐ coughing

# WEAPONS OF MASS DESTRUCTION

Weapons of mass destruction are or are delivered by:

- nuclear explosives
- ballistic missiles
- cruise weapons
- aircraft
- chemical warfare
- biological warfare

} capable of killing tens, hundreds, thousands or millions of people and causing huge damage to buildings and the environment

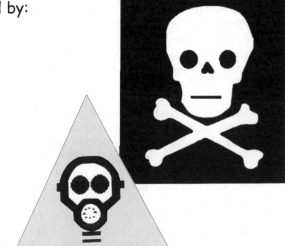

**Nuclear club** = USA, Russia, China, Britain, France, India, Pakistan (have declared nuclear weapons but others may also be capable of making them)

**Chemical weapons** = substances used to harm by working on the body to kill, e.g. nerve agents, blister agents, choking agents (they force the enemy to wear full protective clothing and this makes fighting less effective)

**Biological weapons** = infectious agents such as bacteria or viruses used to harm, e.g. anthrax, yersina pestis (Black Death of 14th century), cholera, typhoid, bubonic plague, cobra venom

The idea of weapons of mass destruction is not modern. Earlier examples:

**429 BC** Spartans set fire to pitch and sulphur to make toxic fumes in Peloponnesian War
**1346** Mongols catapulted plague corpses over walls into Crimea forcing defenders to flee
**WW1** tear gas and chlorine gas used
**WW2** Nazis used Zyklon B in gas chambers to kill concentration camp prisoners
**1962–70** USA used tear gas and defoliants such as Agent Orange in Vietnam
**1987** Iraq used hydrogen cyanide and mustard gas against Kurds

Gulf War 1991: Iraq sent troops into Kuwait and took it over. USA led 32 allies such as Britain, France and Egypt against Iraq in Operation Desert Shield. Iraq pulled out of Kuwait. UN set up UNSCOM to inspect Iraq for weapons of mass destruction.

Equipment used by weapons inspectors
- robot spyplanes (tiny pilotless aircraft, can stay over one place for more than 24 hours)
- nuclear monitoring devices (such as portable gamma radiation detectors)
- commercial spy satellites (high resolution images show buildings in minute detail)
- germ warfare detectors (such as miniature sensors and hand-held nucleic acid analysers)
- cameras (tamper-proof digital cameras)

In 2003 the weapons inspectors left Iraq and the US invaded it to get rid of Saddam Hussein and any possible weapons of mass destruction.

**Write down adjectives (describing words) used on the page to describe the following.**

a) agent _____
b) clothing _____
c) destruction _____
d) venom _____
e) resolution _____
f) Shield _____
g) warfare _____
h) War _____
i) gas _____
j) camp _____
k) plague _____
l) spyplanes _____
m) damage _____
n) corpses _____
o) fumes _____
p) sensors _____

# TERRORISM

**Terrorism** = using fear and violence to try to get what you want

**Terror** = intense, sharp, overpowering fear

**Terrorist** = person who is practising terrorism

An act of violence such as planting a bomb which kills some civilians.

### THE CYCLE OF TERRORISM

Reaction to the bombing is an act of violence such as sending troops into destroy villages of the suspected bombers.

What a brave freedom fighter

What a disgusting terrorist

Terrorist is an emotive word – who you think is a terrorist depends on many things such as your ethnic group, religion, economic and social status, age, sex, country.

EXAMPLES:

11 SEPTEMBER 2001: 19 people hijacked four planes. One plane crashed into paddock. Others flew into twin towers of New York World Trade Centre and Pentagon building in Washington. Over 3000 people were killed. US, led by President Bush, blamed Osama bin Laden, a Muslim whose al Qaeda organisation trained terrorists. US attacked places in Afghanistan because it was thought Osama bin Laden was hiding there. US attack caused fall of Taleban, the Muslim rulers of Afghanistan with shocking record in human rights. US turned attention to Iraq led by dictator Saddam Hussein.

OCTOBER 2002: Bomb exploded at nightclub at Kuta Beach, Bali, Indonesia. About 180 killed. Many injured. Many Australians, one Kiwi killed. Al Qaeda claimed responsibility.

"There is no way you can talk to terrorists. The only thing to do is blast them off the face of the earth."
(A)

"The only way to solve the problem of terrorists is not to capture them and lock them up or kill them but to capture their minds and hearts." (B)

## 1 Circle the best alternative about what Speaker A and B are saying:

a)  exactly the same opinions          b)    some same, some different opinions
c)  exactly the opposite opinions

## 2 In which countries are the following?

a) World Trade Centre _____          b) Bali _____

c) Pentagon _____          d) Palestinian suicide bombers _____

e) hiding place for bin Laden _____

# DRUG TRAFFICKING

- Some top cocaine and heroin producers are Colombia, Bolivia, Peru, Myanmar, Afghanistan. These countries are poor. Growing illicit drugs is a way for poor farmers to make money. They smuggle the drugs into other countries.
- Drug trafficking is a $400 billion per year industry.
- It represents 8% of the world's trade.
- All efforts to stop it have failed.
- Not everyone agrees with the 'drug war' because it focuses on wiping out production in developing countries (supply) rather than sorting out issues in developed countries (demand).

> **trafficking** = dealing in illicit drugs
> **illicit** = illegal
> **opium** = product from poppies = illicit drug
> **morphine** = purified from opium = medicine
> **heroin** = chemical derivative of morphine = illicit drug
> **cocaine** = product of dried coca leaf = illicit drug

**Getting the opium from poppies**
- Poppies flower
- Flowers fall and leave green seed-cases
- Seed-cases are slit and milky juice oozes out
- Juice is collected, dried and pressed into opium cakes

**Getting the cocaine from coca leaves**
- Farmers spread out coca leaves on a tarp to dry
- Dried leaves put into a pit
- Chemicals are added to take out the cocaine alkaloid

**Efforts to stop drug trafficking**
- spraying crops with herbicide (this damages any surrounding rainforest)
- threatening to stop foreign aid to drug-producing countries
- gun battles between farmers and the police/military
- setting fire to heroin labs
- putting farmers in prison until they agree to destroy their crops
- execution (some countries have death penalty for drug trafficking)
- life sentences for drug trafficking

**Main Southeast Asia heroin-trafficking routes**

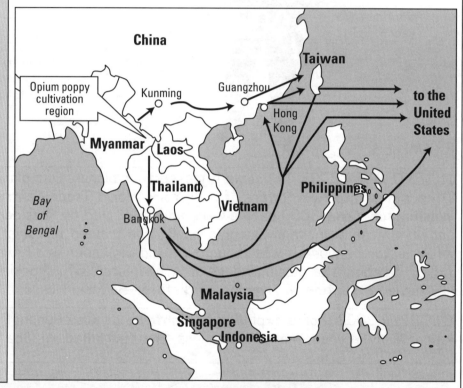

## Check out the map and fill in the gaps.

a) The part of the world shown is called _____.

b) The plant from which opium comes is called _____.

c) The heroin comes from _____, which comes from opium.

d) The main opium cultivation region shown is _____.

e) The word that means "dealing in illicit drugs" is _____.

f) The capital city on a drug trafficking route is _____.

g) Laos also grows a lot of opium and cannabis. It is situated _____ of Myanmar.

h) Myanmar is the world's largest opium producer. A lot of its opium ends up in _____.

i) From Myanmar, drugs go east through _____ to Taiwan.

j) From Thailand, drugs go to _____ and _____ before the US.

**1** "Give me your tired, your poor, Your huddled masses yearning to breathe free, The wretched refuse of your teeming shore, Send these, the homeless, tempest-tossed to me" *from a poem by Emma Lazarus*

**2** **refugees** = homeless people who have lost or fled homes because of war or persecution (not being given equal rights with other groups of people); the word comes from French *refugie*, which means someone who has taken refuge from being chased or other danger

**3** Estimates say there are 14–15 million refugees in the world.

**4** UNHCR = United Nations High Commissioner for Refugees

**5** Causes of refugees:
- war with another country or within a country (civil war)
- famine – no food left in area
- unfair laws forcing people out

**6** Palestinians are refugees:
- they are Arabs who used to live where Israel now is and they fled during the 1948 Arab-Israeli war
- millions live in refugee camps
- Israel has built Jewish settlements in the West Bank and Gaza Strip, which it took after winning a six-day war with its Arab neighbours
- Palestinian intifada (uprising) started in Gaza in 1980s against Israeli rule; present violence includes Palestinian suicide bombings and Israeli troops destroying houses of bombers' families

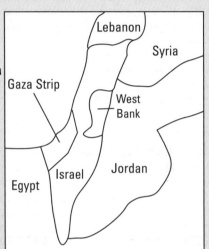

**7** Problems in refugee camps
- poor food or not enough food
- little or unsafe water
- no hope for the future
- no hygiene and sanitation
- overcrowding
- diseases
- no schools
- cycle of violence
- no jobs
- no privacy
- high stress levels
- don't own land

---

**1** Check out the map and then give the names for the following.

a) Six places where Palestinian refugees might live are _____ , _____ , _____ , _____ , _____ , _____ .

b) The two places taken by Israel from the Arab neighbours are _____ and _____ .

c) The place where Palestinians used to live is _____

**2** Write down the numbers of the boxes that match the following.

a) tells you what your life could be like if you were a refugee _____

b) explains an abbreviation _____

c) has a mathematical "best guess" _____

d) gives reasons for **2** _____

e) uses a group as an example _____

f) gives a definition and origin for a word _____

g) would be the one used as an inscription on New York's Statue of Liberty. _____

# EXTREME NATURAL EVENTS

**extreme** = way past being ordinary or normal
**natural events** = processes made by nature and not by humans

- often unpredictable
- strike suddenly
- can cause massive loss of life
- can cause massive property loss
- can traumatise people (upset them so much they can't function properly)

## SOME EXAMPLES:

**1906 San Francisco, USA:** earthquake, destroyed hundreds of buildings, fires swept through city, about 3000 dead and many thousands homeless

**1983 Melbourne, Australia:** dust storm, dumped 320m of thick sand

**1995 Chicago, USA:** tropical heat wave, humidity of 90%, city an oven, extreme temperatures, about 525 people died in several days, intense jungle weather

**1998 Papua New Guinea:** tsunami wave 7–10 m, max height of 15 m, along about 40 km of coastline, wiped out villages in coastal lagoon regions, killed about 3000 people

**AD 79 Mt Vesuvius, Italy:** volcano erupted, destroyed city of Pompeii

**1883 Krakatoa, Indonesia:** volcano caused tsunamis, more than 30,000 people are believed to have died

**2003 Southeast Australia:** drought, parched plains, high winds, terrible forest fires, over 500 houses destroyed, deaths

**1998 Quebec, Canada:** ice storm, waves of freezing rain made layer upon layer of ice on everything from power lines to cows and sugar maple taps, about 1.4 m thick, thousands without electricity for at least a week, people couldn't get to work or school

**2002 Colorado, USA:** fire, blazed across thousands of hectares, thousands of people evacuated

**2002 Queensland, Australia:** lightning killed man working on house roof

**1974 Darwin, Australia:** tropical cyclone (typhoon, hurricane) destroyed city, killed about 66 people

**1943 Seattle, USA:** snowstorm injured 11 children, one child died, schools closed, ferries unable to land marooned passengers, stalled cars blocked streets, overheated furnaces and stoves caused fires

**1947 Oklahoma, USA:** tornado, twisted windmill towers into corkscrew shapes, hurled baths and vehicles the length of a football field into trees, killed 107 people

**1998 Yangtze River, China:** flood, killed over 2500, millions left homeless, rats spread diseases

## 1 Write down to which extreme natural event the following refer.

a) can reach over 30 m high on shore but hard to see in ocean _____

b) quick 'strike without warning' kills about 100 people a year in USA _____

c) oil in eucalypts puts Australian and Californian forests at risk _____

## 2 Write down an extreme natural event that happened in the following places.

a) San Francisco _____   b) Oklahoma _____

c) Seattle _____   d) Papua New Guinea _____

e) Colorado _____   f) Krakatoa _____

g) Darwin _____   h) Yangtze _____

i) Chicago _____

# Unit 41

# EL NINO

**WHAT** temporary change in climate, making unusually warm weather

**WHERE** Pacific in region around equator

**WHY** ocean surface warms up and the place where thunderstorms happen on the equator moves eastward; this sets off changes in weather around the world

**WHEN** every two to seven years and lasts between 12 and 36 months each time

**WHO** El Nino means 'The Little Boy' or 'Christ Child' in Spanish, the language spoken along South America where El Nino first appeared around Christmas

La Nina means The Little Girl. It is the opposite of El Nino. It has unusually cold ocean temperatures in the equatorial Pacific.

**RESULTS**
- drought in some places such as Australia, Indonesia, NZ
- floods in other places such as USA and Peru
- forest fires in some places and ice storms in other places
- famines because of extreme hazards
- death of thousands of people because of extreme natural events
- billions of dollars worth of damage

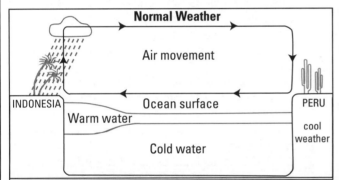

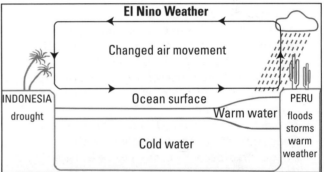

## 1 Colour in the diagram.

## 2 Fill in the gaps in the following called 'My name is El Nino'.

a) In Spanish my name means _____.

b) I turn up once every two to _____ years.

c) I hang around each visit for 12 to _____ months.

d) I live in the ocean, in the region around the _____.

e) My opposite is called _____, which means _____.

f) I'm likely to bring _____ to Indonesia and _____ to Peru.

g) I mess up the _____ climate, not only in the Pacific but in many parts of the _____.

h) Usually warm water piles up in the western part of the Pacific but I pile it up in the _____ part of the _____.

# OZONE HOLE

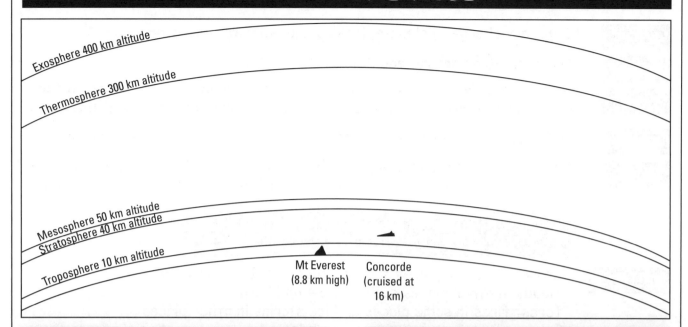

Exosphere 400 km altitude

Thermosphere 300 km altitude

Mesosphere 50 km altitude

Stratosphere 40 km altitude

Troposphere 10 km altitude

Mt Everest
(8.8 km high)

Concorde
(cruised at
16 km)

## ABOUT OZONE

- It's part of the web of life.
- It's a thin layer of gas in the stratosphere.
- It wraps round the Earth.
- It's thinnest in the tropics around the equator and thicker towards the South Pole (Antarctica) and North Pole (Arctic).
- It absorbs some ultraviolet (UV) radiation from the sun. UV can cause skin cancer and damage vegetation.
- It blocks most of the UV reaching Earth.
- Over Antarctica, and recently over the Arctic, stratosphere ozone has been depleted (lessened) at certain times of the year.

## ABOUT THE OZONE HOLE

- Loss of ozone was first seen in the 1970s.
- The ozone hole is not really a hole. It's an area where the ozone layer is so thin that more UV is reaching Earth.
- This is mainly due to the release of manmade chemicals.
- Chlorofluorocarbons (CFCs) are manmade chemicals used to make things such as fridges and air-conditioners. They escape and drift into the upper atmosphere where they destroy the ozone.
- CFC use has declined since a 1987 international agreement to reduce CFC production.

### CLUES
**Across**
1. today ... ozone is reaching Earth
5. around the equator
6. noticed in 1970s
7. the hole is ... really a hole
9. ozone is part of the ... of life
10. hollow place
13. of and about Antarctica
16. sends out UV radiation
18. what ozone is
19. UV can make cancers on this

**Down**
2. layer in the stratosphere
3. Pole where Antarctica is
4. CFCs are ... in fridges
8. ozone ... much UV
9. ozone ... round the Earth
11. CFCs ... upwards
12. opposite of thick
14. it ... longer to get into the stratosphere than the troposhere
15. opposite of thin
17. ultraviolet

# ENDANGERED RAINFOREST AND SPECIES

Animals and plants are divided into groups called species or biodiversity. There is more biodiversity in rainforests than anywhere else on Earth. More than 50% of the world's plant and animal species, including native (indigenous) people, live in rainforests. Scientists are discovering new species all the time.

**endangered** = in danger of becoming extinct = being lost forever

Rainforest and plant and animal species are endangered because:
- people slash and burn forest to make farms and ranches
- taking away forest destroys homes for plants and animals
- outsiders have come to cut trees down for logs
- outsiders have come to mine
- people capture animals to sell as pets.

Rainforests provide:
- oxygen
- beauty
- house plants, e.g. periwinkle
- fruits, e.g. banana, avocado, orange
- additives, e.g. chicle used in chewing gum
- nuts, e.g. cashews, Brazil nuts
- drinks, e.g. coffee beans
- sweets, e.g. chocolate from cacao seed
- oils, e.g. cacao seed oil used in suntan lotion
- filling, e.g. kapok tree produces filling in pillows
- latex from rubber tree, e.g. used in tyres
- 25% of medicines, e.g. quinine to treat malaria
- a valuable 'bank' of rare plants, which will help future scientists make very important new drugs and products.

**About 2000 rainforest trees per minute are cut down**

**1** In the drawing find and colour in the following animals:

Harpy eagle, Howler monkey, Parrot, Orangutan, Boa constrictor, Alligator, Morpho butterfly, Scorpion, Red-eyed tree frog, Leopard

**2** Write down four reasons why the habitat (homes) of rainforest animals and plants is disappearing.

Estimated rate of extinction is 50,000 species every year, an average of about 140 per day; they are disappearing before they can be catalogued and studied

a) _____

b) _____

c) _____

d) _____

# KYOTO AGREEMENT

Before 1997 scientists said:
- gases such as carbon dioxide were increasing because of human actions such as burning oil and coal
- gases were making Earth heat up like a glasshouse and causing global warming
- global warming could be really bad for Earth
- every country should work to cut down on the amount of $CO_2$ it produced.

So, a special conference was held in Kyoto, Japan.

"The US is the world's biggest polluter. Every year it produces enough $CO_2$ to cover the whole US, including Alaska and Hawaii, with a foot of $CO_2$. In 2001 it said it would not be bound by the Kyoto Agreement because it 'is not in the United States' economic best interest'."

**Greenhouse Gases**

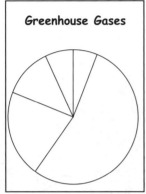

1997 Global Climate Conference was held in the city of Kyoto in Japan. About 160 countries made up the Kyoto Agreement. It said countries would promise to cut down on the amount of $CO_2$ they produced. Countries can sign up to it any time.

"It doesn't do enough."

"It will slow down economic development."

"Demand for cleaner technologies will create new businesses and jobs."

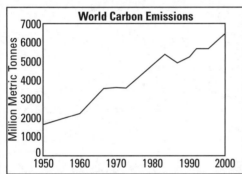

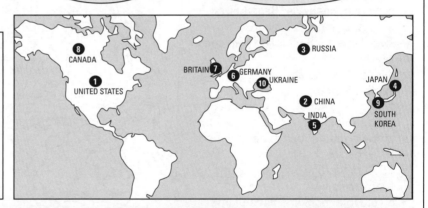

1 **List the top 10 $CO_2$-producing countries in order from biggest to smallest.**

1 _____ 2 _____ 3 _____

4 _____ 5 _____ 6 _____

7 _____ 8 _____ 9 _____

10 _____

2 **Fill in the percentages and names of gases on the graph of Greenhouse Gases.**
**($CO_2$ = 54%, CFCs = 21%, methane = 12%, ozone = 7%, nitrous oxide = 6%)**

3 **Colour the graph of World Carbon Emissions and fill in the following gaps.**

a) Carbon emissions are measured in _____

b) Emissions means _____

c) Emissions went from about _____ metric tonnes in 1950 to about 6500 in _____.

# THE BERMUDA TRIANGLE

The Bermuda Triangle:

- an imaginary triangle with its three points at Miami (mainland US), Bermuda (islands NE of Miami), Puerto Rico (island SE of Miami)

- also known as *Devil's Triangle* and *Hoodoo Sea*

- known for supposedly paranormal ('para' in front of a word means 'beyond') disappearances of boats and planes

- the legend began in 1945 when five military planes and a rescue plane disappeared in the area; later magazines published stories about strange disappearances

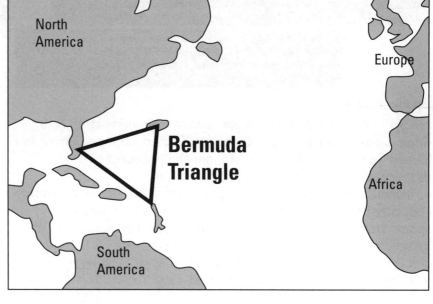

- statistics show it is no more dangerous than other areas of open ocean

- the area is one of two places in the world where a magnetic compass does point towards true north, which can make navigation tricky (the other place is an area often called the 'Devil's Sea', off the east coast of Japan, and it is also known for its mysterious disappearances)

- The Gulf Stream in the area is very swift and rough and can quickly get rid of any evidence of a disaster

- the weather pattern often produces thunderstorms and water spouts, which can bring disaster for pilots and mariners

- the ocean floor varies from shallow to deep and is always changing

- inexperienced boaties and pilots are common in the area. They get into trouble if they travel too far from the coast and don't have enough fuel.

---

**1** On the map of the Bermuda Triangle write in the names of the land that are at the three points.

---

**2** Write down the things that the following words were describing.

|  |  |
|---|---|
| a)  imaginary _____ | b)  Devil's _____ |
| c)  Hoodoo _____ | d)  paranormal _____ |
| e)  strange _____ | f)  magnetic _____ |
| g)  true _____ | h)  tricky _____ |
| i)  Gulf _____ | j)  thunder _____ |
| k)  water _____ | l)  ocean _____ |

# SPACE

Space = that part of the universe that lies outside the Earth's atmosphere, aka outer space; only way to get there is launch spacecraft from Earth by powerful rockets.

Space spin-offs = e.g. joystick controllers used for computer games, originally developed by NASA to use on spaceships to Moon.

Space peace = 1966 Treaty forbids weapon testing in space, orbiting of nuclear weapons round Earth, setting up military bases on Moon or planets.

**Space vocab:**

**NASA** National Aeronautics and Space Administration (US)
**Cape Canaveral** now **Cape Kennedy** (Kennedy Space Centre in Florida)
**launch vehicles** rockets used to launch spacecraft
**astronautics** science of space exploration
**astronauts** space travellers (cosmonauts = Russian astronauts)
**spacecraft** vehicle for space travel (spaceship = spacecraft with crew)
**space station** spaceship or satellite in semi-permanent orbit
**international space station** involves 16 countries and over 100,000 people, first two modules launched and joined together in orbit 1998, first crew arrived 2000
**space shuttle** re-useable spacecraft designed to carry people and gear
**spacesuit** protective garment worn by astronauts
**spacewalkers** astronauts doing tasks outside space station
**payload** load carried in a rocket or satellite
**satellite** device for launching into orbit
**capsule** cabin on spacecraft that contains crew or instruments
**module** detachable section of a spacecraft
**dock** two spacecraft joining in space
**orbit** path followed by spacecraft
*Sputnik 1* first satellite, launched by USSR in 1957
*Apollo 11* US Neil Armstrong first man on Moon 1969
**Challenger** US shuttle, 1986 exploded on lift-off, all seven crew died
**Hubble telescope** lifted into orbit 1990 aboard shuttle *Discovery*
*Columbia* US space shuttle, 2003 broke up over Texas as descended from orbit, all seven crew died.

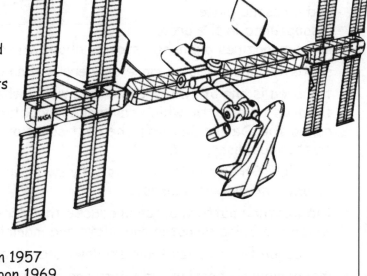

## Write down events that would best match the following.

a) some people say this didn't happen and the US played a trick on the world by saying man walked on this place _____

b) sent magnifying "eyes" into space to learn more space secrets _____

c) tragedy of 1986 _____

d) tragedy of 2003 _____

e) most complex engineering project in the world is taking place in space

_____

f) launched the space age _____

g) approved by the United Nations to keep space peace _____

# OLYMPIC GAMES

### Where the name comes from
The ancient Greek gods lived on Mount Olympus, and Olympia was a plain in Greece where athletic games were held every four years in ancient times. Today's Olympic flame is lit at Olympia, where a flame burned during the ancient games, and taken to host country.

### Prizes
In the ancient games winners got a branch cut with a gold-handled knife from a wild olive tree. Today's winners get gold, silver and bronze medals.

### Olympic motto
"Citius, Altius, Fortius" (Latin for "faster, higher, braver" although the modern translation is "swifter, higher, stronger").

### Olympic rings represent all the continents
Rings are interlaced from left to right: (top) blue, black, red; (bottom) yellow, green.

### Sports
The ancient games had running, wrestling, pentathlon, boxing and a horse chariot race, all for men. A boxing match could last for hours and sometimes men were killed. Running was generally in the nude, although in one race contestants had to run wearing a full set of armour. Today's games have 35 sports and about 400 events. Sports are aquatics, archery, athletics, badminton, baseball, basketball, boxing, canoe/kayak, cycling, equestrian, fencing, football, gymnastics, handball, hockey, judo, modern pentathlon, rowing, sailing, shooting, softball, table tennis, taekwondo, tennis, triathlon, volleyball, weightlifting, wrestling, biathlon, bobsleigh, curling, ice hockey, luge, skating, skiing. The Winter Olympics is for sports practised on snow and ice. The Games are for females as well.

### Olympic spirit
In 1896 Frenchman Baron Pierre de Coubertin started up the modern Olympic Games. He said, "The most important thing in the Games is not winning but taking part." He thought international sports were vital for the mental and physical development of young people; they would help young people from different countries to become friends and this would help build a peaceful and better world. The Olympic spirit is about friendship, solidarity and fair play.

Competition is between athletes, not countries. At the 2000 Games the South and North Korean teams paraded in the stadium together under the flag of the Korean peninsula. They got huge applause.

---

**1** Colour the Olympic rings the right colours.

---

**2** Put two bits together to make words to do with the Olympic Games.

| Cou | pia | ling | ci | thlon | trian | kwondo | tants |
| dium | bob | bertin | Olym | wrest | arity | arc | tae |
| penta | hery | tius | eques | sta | solid | sleigh | contes |

a) _____      b) _____      c) _____

d) _____      e) _____      f) _____

g) _____      h) _____      i) _____

j) _____      k) _____      l) _____

Obesity means being far too overweight.
Millions of people in the world are starving.
Millions of people in the world are sick because
they are too fat.

### Changing body shapes
- A couple of centuries ago, the ideal of a beautiful female body was full-figured. The name given to a full figure is Rubenesque. It comes from the painter Rubens who painted full-bodied women. Plumper people were admired because they showed they were wealthy, being able to afford plentiful food.
- The modern concentration of skinny models helped give rise to eating disorders such as bulimia and anorexia.
- The last huge change in the human shape was about 200 years ago in Europe at the time of the Agricultural Revolution. The average adult height increased by about 30 cm. This was linked to a better diet and health.
- Today the human body is changing shape again. Since 1980 the average man in the world has gone from weighing 74 kilos to 82 kilos. The average woman in the world has gone from weighing 62 kilos to 69 kilos. The major change is an increase in girth. Fatter people have huge consequences for the world.

"If frogs found their food piled up on lily-pads without having to be caught, they'd get fat too."
World expert on obesity

### Problems associated with obesity
- breathing problems
- musculo-skeletal problems
- skin problems
- infertility (unable to have children)
- diabetes
- gall bladder disease
- high blood pressure
- stroke, coronary heart disease
- parents outliving their obese children

### Causes of increasing numbers of obese people
- people doing less physical activity than in the past
- food is more easily available
- people doing less physical leisure activities
- fatty junk food is readily available and appealing
- massive advertising for 'junk food'

### Simple cures for obesity
- do more physical activity
- avoid junk food (eating it now and again is much better than living on it)

## 1 Number 1 to 4 in order of thinnest to fattest.

☐ overweight     ☐ underweight     ☐ obese     ☐ average weight

## 2 Write down four causes of obesity.

a) _____     b) _____

c) _____     d) _____

## 3 Write down four possible health problems caused by obesity.

a) _____     b) _____

c) _____     d) _____

# Unit 49

# LIFE EXPECTANCY

these terms help describe the health of a population

## Examples of global life expectancy

1950     46 years
2000     65 years
2050     77 years
(Before the Industrial Revolution of the 18th century, global life expectancy was maybe 20–30 years)

**mortality** = death
**morbidity** = sickness
**disability** = not at full strength
**life expectancy** = the average number of years a baby born at a certain time in a certain country is likely to live

## Causes of increasing life expectancy

- better nutrition (diet)
- family planning
- reduction in diseases
- education
- inventions of medicines
- technological advances

## Examples of today's life expectancy

| | |
|---|---|
| Afghanistan | 47 |
| Australia | 80 |
| Ethiopia | 44 |
| Japan | 81 |
| NZ | 78 |
| Russia | 68 |

## Examples of life expectancy at certain times

- 1540 English government guessed it was 7 years for England
- late 1700s English government guessed it was 14 years for England
- Early Maori = about 25–30
- 1830 for factory workers in Bolton, England = 17 years
- 1900 for USA = 47 years

## Health hints for a good life expectancy

- Don't smoke
- Don't eat much fast food and convenience food
- Drink alcohol in moderation
- Be careful in the sun – slip on T-shirt, slop on sunscreen, slap on hat, wrap sunglasses
- Try to say unstressed
- Try to get regular, decent sleep
- Do regular exercise – any sort of movement helps, such as skateboarding or car washing

## Top 10 health risks globally

- Childhood underweight
- High blood pressure
- Heavy alcohol use
- Lack of hygiene and sanitation
- Indoor smoke from solid fuels
- Obesity (being overweight)
- Unsafe sex
- Smoking
- Unsafe water
- High cholesterol

**1** Tick or cross the boxes to show if the following are good or bad for a reasonable life expectancy.

 a) [ ]

 b) [ ]

 c) [ ]

 d) [ ]

 e) [ ]

 f) [ ]

 g) [ ]

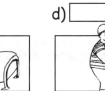 h) [ ]

 i) [ ]

j) [ ]

**2** Write down the terms on the page that mean the following.

a) death _____

b) sickness _____

c) not at full strength _____

d) diet _____

e) free from germs _____

f) staying healthy _____

g) average number of years a baby is likely to live _____

# EXAMPLES OF INSPIRATIONAL PEOPLE

**Dalai Lama** (1935 –)
Head of State and spiritual leader
of Tibetan people. Lives as simple Buddhist monk.
China invaded Tibet in 1950. Dalai Lama escaped to
India where he now lives. Won Nobel Peace Prize.
Works for world peace, free Tibet, human rights in
Tibet, to stop China using Tibet for nuclear weapons
production and nuclear waste dump. Says: "Our
struggle must remain non-violent and free of hatred."

**New York firefighters**
One day in September 2001 terrorists
crashed two hijacked planes into the two
towers of the World Trade Centre in New
York. When the planes crashed, enormous
fireballs erupted as fuel exploded and
burned. Firefighters were sent in to help
save people trapped in the burning towers.
When the buildings collapsed, many
thousands of people died, including 343
firefighters. For many weeks, other
firefighters searched rubble for survivors.
This area became known as Ground Zero.
One photograph became a symbol of this
time. It shows three heroic dust-covered
firefighters raising the American flag in
the middle of all the chaos and disaster.
They sent a message to the world that hope
had survived.

**Sister Teresa** (1910–97)
Born in Macedonia. Went to
India as missionary. Found a
dying woman 'half eaten by maggots and rats' lying in a
Calcutta street, sat with her until the woman died. From
then on she spent every day caring for poor and unloved.
Called The Saint of the Gutters and Angel of Mercy.
Won Nobel Peace Prize. In Beirut rescued 37 children
trapped in hospital by getting temporary ceasefire
between Israeli army and Palestinian guerrillas. Said: "If
we worry too much about ourselves, we won't have time
for others" and "Peace begins with a smile."

**Nelson Mandela** (1918 –)
Black South African.
Worked against apartheid
where whites, minority race,
kept most land and power. When his
organisation was outlawed, he had to live
apart from his family and disguised himself
to escape government informers and spies.
When he was arrested Mandela was
sentenced to life imprisonment. Spent many
years in Robben Island prison. Released 1990.
Won Nobel Peace Prize. First democratically
elected President of South Africa.

**Princess Diana** (1961–97)
Born Lady Diana Frances Spencer in
England. Married Prince Charles.
Divorced. Sons are Prince William
and Prince Harry. Famous for her style. Killed in car
accident. Remembered for charity work for arts, sick,
children, disabled. Tried to get land mines banned.

## Give the names of the following mentioned by name.

a)   The person who did not get the Nobel Peace Prize _____

b)   The American object that is most likely to be called Old Glory _____

c)   The region where the World Trade Centre used to be _____

d)   The old system of government in South Africa _____

e)   The city in India which became Sister Teresa's adopted home _____

f)   The country which now rules Tibet _____

g)   The country in which the Dalai Lama lives _____

# FINAL CHALLENGE

1     The original Jack-o-lantern was in a turnip / pumpkin.
2     The Muslim God is known as Mohammed / Allah.
3     The capital of Vietnam is Hanoi / Kampuchea.
4     Africa is separated from Europe by the Mediterranean Sea / Indian Ocean.
5     The largest ocean in the world is the Pacific / Atlantic.
6     The Kyoto Agreement is about rice crops / greenhouse gases.
7     The skullcap worn by Jews is a yarmulk / bindi.
8     An eating disorder is Rubenesque / bulimia.
9     Polynesia means many islands / little islands.
10    The number of Olympic rings is five / seven.
11    Being hugely overweight is infertility / obesity
12    Bali's Kuta Beach is in Indonesia / India.
13    The *Kursk* was a nuclear submarine / reactor.
14    The 'father of Communism' was Stalin / Lenin.
15    War within a country is called civil / cold.
16    UNSCOM was aimed at Israel / Iraq.
17    The Punjab is a state in India / Nepal.
18    The Chechens are fighting against Turkey / Russia.
19    Spanish for Little Boy weather is La Nina / El Nino.
20    The religion of Guy Fawkes was Catholic / Protestant.
21    Dolly was a cloned goat / sheep.
22    Saddam Hussein is most associated with Russia / Iraq.
23    In 1883 Krakatoa in Indonesia suffered a volcano / tsunami.
24    The medicine purified from opium is heroin / morphine.
25    The parliament known as the Knesset is in Israel / Hong Kong.
26    Ceylon is now called Sri Lanka / Argentina.
27    Someone in favour of the Royal Family is a republican / monarchist.
28    A government with a religious group in power is a theocracy / tyranny.
29    Perfect peace with no suffering is nirvana / saffron.
30    The capital of Germany is Copenhagen / Bonn.
31    CER is for China and Russia / Australia and NZ.
32    The Balkans jut into the Mediterranean / Barents.
33    The country suspended from ANZUS is NZ / Australia.
34    Creutzfeldt-Jakob Disease strikes humans / animals.
35    Osama bin Laden is associated with Holy See /al Qaeda.
36    The Taj Mahal is in India / Tangiers.
37    The number of permanent UN Security Council members is 5 / 15.
38    The Kalahari in Africa is a basin / desert.
39    The ancient Roman god of love was Cupid / Rhea.
40    The capital of Scotland is Cardiff / Edinburgh.
41    The Hindu Festival of Lights is Ganesha / Divali.
42    The religion of Muslims is called Islam / Sikhism.
43    The largest part of Ireland is N. Ireland / Republic of Ireland.
44    Israel was created as a modern country in 1948 / 1998.
45    The modern Olympic Games were begun in 1896 by a Frenchman / Greek.
46    Hatred of Jews is anti-semitism / bar mitzvah.
47    Ozone is found in the thermosphere / stratosphere.
48    The patron saint of Ireland is St Patrick / St Andrew.
49    Terrorist attacks on USA took place on 11 September 1999 / 2001.
50    A gurdwara is a Sikh temple / Hindu shrine.

51     The Warsaw Pact was for communist countries / democratic countries.
52     The three-leaved clover is called leprechaun / shamrock.
53     Big Brother stands for a forum / dictator.
54     The Tsar and Tsarina were leaders of Afghanistan / Russia.
55     A prince of a Muslim country is called emir / eritrea.
56     In 1906 San Francisco suffered a hurricane / an earthquake.
57     Known as 'the rich man's club' is the OECD / G77.
58     An old word for holy is celtic / hallow.
59     The Kremlin is in Moscow / Bangkok.
60     Buddha is The One Who Travels / The One Who Knows.
61     Eskimos are Inuit / Sanskrit.
62     The Bermuda Triangle is known as Devil's Armpit / Hoodoo Sea.
63     Siam is the old name for Thailand / Laos.
64     1939-45 was the time of World War 1 / World War 2.
65     Richer countries are known as The North / The South.
66     The Family of Nations refers to the Pacific Forum / Commonwealth.
67     Believers in Jesus as the Son of God are Jews / Christians.
68     SARS is a virus / space station.
69     Arbor is Latin for tree / Labour.
70     Cane toad and cassowary are found in Australia / NZ.
71     The capital of Bosnia is Herzegovina / Sarajevo.
72     The AP in APEC stands for Asia Pacific / Associated Polynesia.
73     President Milosevic was from Cambodia / Yugoslavia.
74     The capital of Northern Ireland is Dublin / Belfast.
75     Valentine's Day is 14 February / 25 April.
76     Geneva is in The Netherlands / Switzerland.
77     Operation Desert Shield was war against Kuwait / Iraq.
78     The island to the east of Africa is Madagascar / Sahara.
79     Intifada is the Palestinian uprising / West Bank government.
80     Antarctic refers to the North Pole / South Pole.
81     The Hindu god Shiva is The Life Giver / The Destroyer.
82     In Ancient Greece Olympia was a plain / river.
83     The religion of the Jews is Judaism / Jesuits.
84     The Muslim Holy Book is the Koran / Mosque.
85     Iraq used mustard gas against Kurds / Palestinians.
86     The science of space exploration is Canaveral / astronautics.
87     The capital of Syria is Damascus / Jerusalem.
88     Saddam Hussein was leader of Iraq / Kuwait.
89     The majority religion in Northern Ireland is Protestantism / Catholicism.
90     The British Royal Family is Whitehall / Windsor.
91     The Kruger National Park is in South Africa / Pakistan.
92     Mecca and Medina are in Yemen / Saudi Arabia.
93     The Untouchables are also called Dalit / Mantra.
94     The US used Agent Orange in Vietnam / Vatican City.
95     Hinduism began in Peru / India.
96     GE and GM are the same thing / totally different things.
97     Wire and a candle is a symbol for Amnesty International / European Union.
98     The House of Lords and House of Commons are in Canberra /London.
99     Pol Pot was a tyrant in Cambodia / Israel.
100    The world's nuclear club numbers 7 / 27.